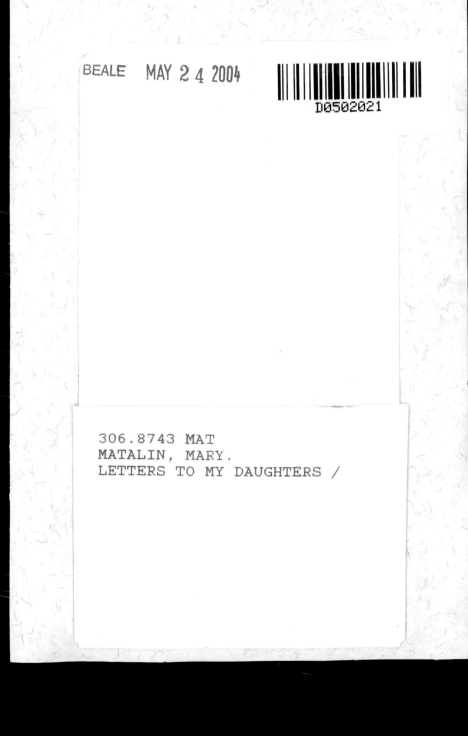

Also by Mary Matalin

All's Fair: Love, War, and Running for President

Matty and Emma Carville, 2003.

LETTERS TO
MY DAUGHTERS

Mary Matalin

SIMON & SCHUSTER
New York   London   Toronto   Sydney

SIMON & SCHUSTER
Rockefeller Center
1230 Avenue of the Americas
New York, NY 10020

SIMON & SCHUSTER and colophon are registered trademarks
of Simon & Schuster, Inc.

For information regarding special discounts for bulk purchases,
please contact Simon & Schuster Special Sales:
1-800-456-6798 or business@simonandschuster.com

Designed by Katy Riegel

Manufactured in the United States of America

10   9   8   7   6   5   4   3   2   1

Library of Congress Cataloging-in-Publication Data is available.

ISBN 0-7432-5608-5

*My grandmother, Irene Gibbs Emerson; my mother, Eileen Emerson Matalin;
my father, Steven G. Matalin; and my grandmother, Helen Tomasevich Matalin;
August 1951.*

Dedicated to my grandmothers,
HELEN TOMASEVICH MATALIN and
IRENE GIBBS EMERSON

And you must tell the child
The legends I told you—
As my mother told them to me and her mother to her.
You must tell the fairy tales of the old country
You must tell of those not of the earth
Who live forever in the hearts of people.
                    —Betty Smith, American writer

CONTENTS

CONTENTS

ACKNOWLEDGMENTS

The last thing I wanted to do when I left the White House in President Bush's midterm was write a book, which I find is like giving birth without an epidural. Especially since 9/11, I'd been tense and distracted, always on the phone or with my nose in some book on Mideast policy. My precious girls, two and five years old when I went to work for the White House, had adjusted to my long days, gone days, and nights of stupor, but I really missed *them*. I was looking forward to full-time mommyhood, taking a break, slowing down.

I wasn't home one week when our old buddy and Simon & Schuster bigwig David Rosenthal called. "You need to write a book—a thoughtful, forward-looking, *big* book on politics, the Republican Party, policy."

"I need to get some sleep," I protested. Nonetheless, knowing he would choose a yummy, expensive restaurant, I agreed to meet him and our attorney and friend, Bob Barnett, for (a free) lunch. My husband, James, joined to help me decline the ever-persuasive Rosenthal (and also to get a free one on David).

I rehearsed all my arguments with James against writing a big book, little book, or anything in between. I ordered a lovely (and costly) chardonnay and launched into them with David. "I can't think, I can't write about politics right now. I *only* care about my daughters. I have no inspiration in me for anything else but them."

"Great! Done!" said David.

"Great! I'll send you some paper," said Bob.

"*What?*" I said.

"Whatcha y'all talkin' 'bout?" said James as he returned from table-hopping.

And that's why you gotta love David and Bob. David insisted that a book to and for my daughters would be cathartic and personally rewarding, *and* a great keepsake for them. And amazingly, Bob got David to actually pay me to create the keepsake! Thanks to both of them for getting the book on track and keeping it there, which turned out to be no small feat.

First off, I am not the most organized gal and my computer skills extend solely to e-mail. Worse, I have zero long-term memory, so my book construct of pulling out stories about my mother for my daughters from my youth sounded good in concept but threatened to be disastrous in execution. The task would have been impossible without my sainted sister, Irene—Renie—O'Brien. Renie coauthored, copiloted, and mood-stabilized me every day. She had the razor-sharp memory I lacked. Through this book, we laughed and cried and relived our sisterhood. I have too much to love about Renie and no words to thank her for this gift we made for our kids.

Renie did get us going, but not even a saint could deal with the rapid succession of wholly disorienting, unexpected events as our deadline approached: a family death, a family accident of devastating magnitude, the flooding of our brand-new house—to cite just a few of the incidents that uprooted our routine and ripped out our hearts. With a heavy spirit, I told David I couldn't finish the book. It was mostly written but totally unedited and I had too many more pressing responsibilities to complete it. Nothing fazes David. He went out and coerced an incredible woman to coerce me into bringing the book across the finish line. Betsy Rapoport, mother, wife, gourmet chef, stand-up comic, religious tutor, preteen counselor, and editor extraordinaire, had not a speck of time in her overfilled life for another project. So she quit sleeping. She took a landfill of unconnected pages and magically converted them into an actual, readable product, on time. More, she was/is a soul sister of the first order—comforting, understanding, hilarious, brilliant. She even loaned me her perfect mom, Big Moo (don't ask), for Christmas cheer. At least once a day my mom said, "Everything happens for a reason," and the reason for the book became meeting Betsy Rapoport. Life would be ashes in my mouth without her.

Weirdly, a big help on a book from mothers to daughters came from a dad, Jon Macks, who gave me good advice and great one-liners; he's alarmingly calming for being so anal-retentive.

And of course, the girls' dad, my truly amazing-in-so-many-ways husband, put up with my emotional outbursts throughout the entire project. James is a good man and a very good father.

Thanks and apologies to Kerri Kolen for all the under-the-gun assignments. She is the best. And thanks to Lisa Healy, whose super anal-retentiveness thrilled my sister. And, as always, to Kelly Campbell, whose pictorial chronicles of our family never fail to hug our hearts.

David was so right. Trying to pass on your mother's wisdom to your own daughters is truly cathartic. I loved my mother more than anything but only truly came to understand her and what she meant to me by revisiting how she mothered me. So to my mother, whom I never thanked enough, now in sweet peace, thank you.

Most of all the other beautiful things in life come in twos and threes, by dozens and hundreds. Plenty of roses, stars, sunsets, and rainbows . . . but only one mother in the whole world.
—Kate Douglas Wiggin (1856–1923)

XOXO,
Mary

LETTERS TO
MY DAUGHTERS

My mother, Eileen Emerson Matalin, and my grandmother,
Irene Gibbs Emerson, circa 1941.

INTRODUCTION

Dear Precious Angels,

Today is your mother's fiftieth birthday. My mother died one month after her fiftieth birthday, three weeks after she was hospitalized for a cancer that had metastasized beyond any hope of cure. I was shocked, devastated, inconsolable. At age twenty-six, I was far too young to lose my mother. We were best friends, constant companions. I could not cope with the grief. To avoid dealing with such unexpected, uncontrollable anguish, I began a career at warp speed, with no plans or any idea what to do with my brand-new political science degree. My only goal was to leave *no space* for the choking pain and grief. My unguided missile of a life did not include plans for kids.

Fifteen years (and many adventures) later, I got pregnant (not a minute too soon at age forty-one). The thrill and joy of pregnancy brought with them a fresh stab of missing my mom. But this was more than grief; it was pure terror. How could I have a baby without my mother? What did I know about mothering? Why hadn't I paid more attention to her when she was there to teach me?

I devoured all the so-called child-rearing books, by everyone from time-tested white-haired doctors to trendy baby whisperers. As I pored over these books, suddenly Ma *was* there to save me again. She came alive again through her mother wisdom, which came flooding back to me in her own words—all the common sense she passed on to me, which she always said she got from her own mother, who got it from her mother, and on and on, deep into the roots of our family tree. While those books steeled my courage for your coming (new motherhood can be petrifying), none of them—for that matter, not even all of them combined—came close to equaling my mother's comprehensive catalogue of wise and practical guidelines for leading a good and true life. I could hear her voice letting loose with those quirky little mom sound bites that made me roll my eyes when I was your age, the way you both already do when you tell me, "Mom, you're *embarrassing* me."

Ma's basic philosophy for raising kids was an easy blend of Ben Franklin and the Bible. She was a catalogue of cliches:

A penny saved is a penny earned.

A stitch in time saves nine.

Spare the rod, spoil the child.

The harder you work, the luckier you get.

Let him who is without sin cast the first stone.

Okay, let's talk about the eye rolls. I used to think Ma's sayings were just corny. I know better now, and so will you. To this day, your Aunt Renie, Uncle Steve, and I unconsciously quote Ma to you and your cousins. So whether you realize it or not, you are already linked into the chain of generational wisdom.

You roll your eyes now, but I promise you, darlings, throughout your lives you will often revisit and rely on this aged, earthy insight. It will guide your actions, decisions, and relationships. It will ground and propel you as you pursue your unique potentials. It will provide a source of support and strength when you need to solve problems. It will be your frame of reference as you figure out how to contribute to your community and country.

Though Ma often reduced her profoundly wise insights to commonsense quips, each one was merely a shorthand introduction to a lifelong conversation— mother-daughter soul-searching and sharing. We girls are having some of these chats now on love, loss, good and evil; on clothes, boys, hair and makeup; on school and community; on friends, family, and faith. On you . . . the very special you. But you two are only beginning to experience life's many treasures and disappointments. You are tormented by today's ugly terrors and inspired by rainbows and sleepovers. Your questions are endless; most times you deem my answers senseless. Trust me; your questions won't ever stop, but this mother wisdom will help you find your own answers.

I used to tell my mother and myself, whenever she would heap praise and encouragement on me, "Your opinion doesn't count. You're gonna think I'm great no matter what." Matty and Emma, you already say the same thing to me. So I want to tell you something I didn't understand until many years after my mom was gone. First, no one's opinion counts more than your mom's. It's the one that will ring in your ears and hide in your subconscious, guide you forward and stop you from backsliding. Lift you up and cushion your falls. For good or ill for the rest of your lives.

Second, no one else, *ever*, will think you're great no matter what. Not the way your mother does.

You will value the opinions of many, and many, many, many will think you're great (because you are), but when you have to dig the deepest to find the best and strongest that you are, you will always find your mother sitting in your soul.

I know this so profoundly and completely because it is only in my soul that I can speak to my mother. I pray every day that I can be your best mom for all time. Someone you can lean on for today's stubbed toe and tomorrow's bruised ego. Someone who can make sure that that laugh-out-loud glee that came with your first extraordinary, training-wheel-free, two-wheeler experience is there for all your life experiences to come.

I began writing to you two lambs before you were born. My letters took on a new urgency when my work turned to the evil we all face today and a new seriousness of purpose when my age forced me to think about whether I would be here for your tomorrows. Much to my joy, I found my mother's voice coming through in all those letters. You hear that same voice in your own mother's every day.

I wrote these letters to preserve those voices and our guidance for your lives. I hope that one day you'll pass them on, with your own mother wisdom, to your own kids.

Nobody knows better than your mother—because I said so! And to start, here's the truest piece of wisdom I can pass on to you: You will never know a greater joy or a deeper love than the love you have for your children.

I love you,
Mom

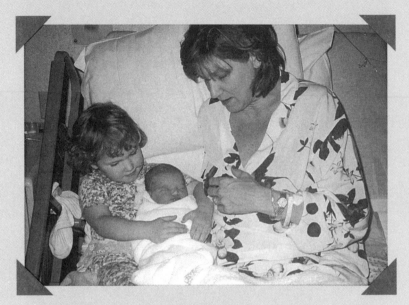

Myself, Matty, and Emma
on the day of Emma's birth,
April 17, 1998.

In the Beginning

Dear Bambinas,

The Humphrevilles joined us for a vacation with their nine-month-old. Georgie gurgles, swiggles, and smiles *a lot*. You two cannot leave him alone. You sit cross-legged on the floor with him or at his feet when he's in the stroller, displaying a patience and attention span normally reserved only for Hilary Duff movies. You repeatedly respond to the baby's infectious squeals of delight by stroking his cottony, coppery wisps of hair.

I'm amazed and amused at the endless extent to which "Carrot Head," as Emma calls him, enraptures you both. At your instinctive gentle touch, your untrained but pitch-perfect cooing and *aahing*, your drop-everything concerned caresses when Georgie appears anywhere near crying.

Where does this come from? Your innate mother knowledge? Your automatic maternal touch? It certainly doesn't come from me. I never liked or wanted kids. I remember babysitting only once, and that was under parental duress when Dad and Ma wanted to go out with my uncle Joe and aunt Mary Ann, who had four towheads spaced less than two years apart. Aunt Mar knew me well enough to have them all asleep before I got there. One of my best friends when I was young was one of nine; never did any of the many little ones engage even my passing attention. I had no dolls or desire for any except Patti Playpal, because she was a giant three feet tall, not a doll at all, but sized to be a real imaginary friend!

The me-first, I-am-woman-hear-me-roar culture of my teens confirmed my early conviction that kids were not for me. Then came college, the chaos of campaigns, career chasing, and never-ending adventures. I surrounded myself with a circle of friends equally uninterested in procreating. In my last and deepest campaign immersion, plastered prominently behind by desk was the poster that read, "Oops, I Forgot to Have Kids," like I cared, which I didn't. The only nag of concern, and it was recessed very deeply in the back of my mind, came when Barbara Bush addressed the Wellesley grads in 1990. I was thirty-seven years old and had reached my all-time professional political apex as the Bush/Quayle deputy campaign manager. Really, it was more than professional: I was blindly passionate about politics in general, George Herbert Walker Bush, specifically. I was completely fulfilled.

Nonetheless, Mrs. Bush broke into my frenetic, totally self-absorbed, purposeful psyche when she told these young women that "at the end of your life, you will never regret not having passed one more test, not winning one more verdict, or not closing one more deal. You will regret time not spent with a husband, a friend, a child, or a parent." In the haze of time, I've come to call this precise moment my awakening. But in real life, real time, few moments are precise, and awakenings are more like gently stirring currents than jolting lightning bolts.

Maybe Mrs. Bush's speech focused me because it came from the most fulfilled, satisfied, complete woman I had ever known. With all she had done, seen, and produced, she ranked her family first. I found this disconcerting, disquieting because making a family was not even on my radar screen. It simply hadn't occurred to me that *anything* could be better than what I was doing. She made me stop and think that there might be *some* merit to settling down for *some* people—but not *me*. I didn't change my ways. Not when we lost the '92 Bush reelection campaign, which derailed me from any career track I might have been on; not when my biological clock chimed forty; not when I married.

At least, nothing consciously changed, but the seed Mrs. Bush unwittingly planted in the back of my thick head must have been setting its own roots. Within five months of marrying, I was pregnant—*accidentally*. Believe me, girls, no fast-paced forty-one-year-old gets pregnant unintentionally. Some force beyond my ken was at work.

Still, my first reaction was horror, shock, disbelief, incredulity. For maybe, oh, twenty minutes. Then I was sledgehammered between the eyes and I took a full-fledged fall into ecstasy. Daddy and I were obsessed, overjoyed; we'd been touched by a miracle. And then I miscarried. Daddy drove in alone with his despair to pick me up at the hospital. We retreated to the mountain house, where we couldn't bring ourselves to leave the loft. We drank a lot of red wine, weeping and wallowing in what seemed to us a singular sorrow.

Don't ever discount miscarriages as insignificant, passing events. I was stunned at the insensitivity of the many who, in one way or another, expressed a dismissive and obligatory sympathy, as if I'd passed a kidney stone! As if the teeny tiny pulsing heart inside me had never beaten. Only other parents who miscarried had an inkling of our painful reality.

As your pregnancies will reveal to you, (1) you know almost instantly that your body is not alone, and (2) your love for that bud, that speck is primal, protective, pervasive, and possessive. When that all-encompassing obsession with another being—*baby*—is suddenly, unexpectedly, inexplicably ended with no being, *no baby*, well, girls, suffice to say, it is *not* a nonevent. Pregnancy, new life, is poignant from the first precious second. Even a joyful birth doesn't erase the pain of an earlier miscarriage.

I'm recounting this sorry episode here to encourage your heartfelt empathy toward miscarrying mothers. I pray you will never need it for yourselves.

I had to discover my baby love later in life and first through grief. But you, beloved bambinas, are blessed to have so automatic and authentic a baby love so early. Your natural affections remind me of my mom. She couldn't get enough of babies, any baby. She remained entranced for hours—playing "Itsy-Bitsy Spider" and peekaboo, making funny faces, rocking, singing—happily lost in some magic maternal world. In the days before endless food scares and the vogue for vegetarianism, she would put me, Aunt Renie, and Uncle Stevie in the middle of a blanket on the floor, give us each a piece of *raw* bacon, and watch us gnaw and squish and spread greasy goo all over our delighted selves. (We kids gag at this memory!)

Ma's undiluted, superstrength mother love only came gushing out of me when you two came into my world. So, little pleases me more than watching it flow so naturally and abundantly from you at so budding an age, knowing you already know the blessing of babies.

Maybe it's your prodigious baby lust or a passing phase (I hope not), but talking about babies is one of your favorite pastimes. I answer all your questions, no matter how advanced. You have all the facts, but the *feelings* associated with motherhood can never be adequately described; you can only live it. Of course, the most indescribable of experiences is actually having a baby—growing a baby inside you and coaxing it out of your own body.

If motherhood is in your future, you will, as all women do, have your own unique birthings, and as unique to you as they will be, birthing will catapult you into the universe of Motherland, where understanding is immediate. All mothers love to tell and hear birthing stories over and over and over. Sipping our wine as the iridescent red Tuscan sun set, Georgie's mom and I detailed ours at such length and with such graphic language that your father had to leave the patio. He harks back to that generation when men didn't share in such recounting; it was unheard of for them to be present for the actual birth! In old movies you'll see the expectant fathers pacing like caged animals around the waiting rooms, grasping a handful of cigars for dear life, barely concealing their "unmanly" anxiety. Today expectant fathers *make* movies in the delivery room! Your dad made the leap into this century by being in the room when you each were born, but he didn't stray one inch from the head of the bed. He said he wanted to steer clear of the "action end."

His natural, limitless hyperactivity combined with inconsolable concern about me *and* his baby made him as close to crazy in my first sweaty contractions as I've ever seen. He was so bad during the throes of the worst stages of my labor with Matty that I asked if they would give *him* an epidural! My epidural was heavy, so my labor was light. I respect women who go for "natural" births, but I told my doctor I didn't consider pain natural: load me up!

I'll spare you the blow-by-blows. Matty was out in three pushes; Emma, one and a half. I was immediately overwhelmed with a sense of relief, exuberance, and a thousand other emotions I can't ever describe.

Daddy went wild, abandoned his post for the "action end" and screamed, *"It's a baby! It's a baby!"* Even through my fog of joy and drugs, I was dimly aware of the reaction from the doctor and nurses to this curious outburst. As in, "What were you expecting? A puppy?" Daddy continued to yip around like a puppy himself until he was handed each of you. He became instantly as still as you have never and will never see him outside of this special situation, immobilized by joy and fear over your tiny newness.

Later, at each birth, the girls—Aunt Renie, Maria, Jill, Gracie—came up with red wine and champagne. When Emma was born, two-year-old Matty came up into our bed, her expression of awe and love captured by Aunt Gracie, the official photo chronicler of all cool events. Most touching to me—and I'll never forget it—was that none of my girlfriends had given birth, yet they each cooed over each of you as if *they* had just delivered you. We were totally tapped into the miracle and each other.

Also unforgettable is the fact that only Aunt Renie knew what to do and what was going on—from how to nurse to how not to panic over your first poops, which I thought were hot tar!

I have relived countless times and reveled in every precious minute of those hours preceding and following your births. They are such a deep part of me that I don't know if I could share them even if I could describe them. But equally gratifying are the moments I remember here: the first time you met your dad, your aunts, your sister. The only thing even remotely as beautiful as your births was how you created a family.

For all time, you are the greatest joy.

XOXO,
Mom

BOYS, PART ONE

Dear Little Flirts,

From my earliest memories, I was fascinated by boys. I think my mother mistook my boy obsession for boyfriend obsession. Boyfriends were fine, but what I really wanted was to be able to do all the things boys were allowed to do.

My parents must have been expecting a boy; they named me Mary Joe after their best friend, Joe Kaminski. Because there were no girls of the right age in my immediate neighborhood, I only hung out with boys. This was before Gloria Steinem and those feminists who wanted to *be* boys. I just wanted to have the same fun and adventures boys had.

Ma and I would spend hours talking about boys. Her overriding theme on the subject was that boys and girls are different. My mother just wanted me not to get in trouble. In those days, "getting in trouble" meant getting pregnant.

Coming from that perspective, my mom was trying to bang into my brain that boys and girls were way different when it came to relationships. She was talking about *girls with boys*. I was more interested in *girls in a boys' world*. They are distinct but parallel tracks of thought. Either way you need to grasp the basic concept that boys come from another place (maybe another planet) and have a distinct world view, disparate priorities and attitudes. They share your vocabulary, but it's not always clear what they truly mean.

When you engage with boys (and men) in whatever situation—dating, working, hanging out—just operate from this categorical concept. You will have more fun, less frustration, and most important, *control*. Control is important with boys (and the men who stay boys).

Boys have their own set of complications, but they are basically simple creatures. Fortunately, you don't need to understand them completely in the way you need to know yourself. You can appreciate, respect, love, and accept them as fellow human beings if you *never, ever* forget that boys and girls are different. This is a good thing; consider it a lifelong adventure to figure out, deal with, and accept this basic concept. Don't fight it.

Up until very recently, you girls perceived little difference between the species. You've both been blessed to have great boys in our neighborhood and school and have learned early that boys can be dear and important friends.

But once you got into nursery school, the very real gender differences began to manifest themselves. Your classes began to self-segregate. The boys had no interest in the play kitchens or dolls, while in your world, dinosaurs, cowboys, and toy soldiers lost their appeal. The boys were running around and shouting while you were playing dress-up and twirling in front of the mirrors. The girls were asking questions while the boys were making faces.

And so it begins—the great mystery of men. You will never fully understand them.

You will develop your own boy theories as you discover yourselves and as your boyfriends multiply. (I remember thinking boys had a special gene for comedy. They could always tell funnier jokes. Oddly, the older they get, the dumber their jokes.) Moreover, since boys control most of the levers of life outside home, it's good to know how they think. To get you started, here's a primer: I should note that since I've been with Daddy for so long, my analysis may be skewed by his omnipresence. But he's a fairly typical male—albeit a *real extreme version* of one. (And he does have more than a few characteristics that are neither male nor female; they're intergalactic—another topic.)

Since you have my female genes, you will likely eschew safe and boring boys for the rowdy and interesting ones. So here's what you can expect in your dealings with boys: Boys are the best and the worst. Boys are exhilarating and exasperating. A boy can be, at any given time, with no notice, a genius or a total butthead, thoroughly sincere or flagrantly opportunistic. To paraphrase Truman Capote, when boys are good, they're very, very good; when they're bad, they're very, very bad.

On a bad day, the best ones have been spoiled by their mothers. Few actually attain maturity or self-control. They have no concept of being gripped by guilt, moodiness, insecurity, or the misery of bad hair days, fat thighs, or having absolutely nothing to wear. They aren't inspired by shopping, chocolate, or romantic movies. They can know and recite every baseball statistic of every player of both leagues going back decades but will forget your birthday. Their idea of a deep, fulfilling conversation is one that is completed in the span of a commercial break (during which time they are switching channels). They cannot cry on command and are immune to nuance or intuition. They can be self-centered, self-absorbed, and downright selfish.

On a good day, their mommas raised them right. They are inspired adventurers and risk takers. They are thrilled by harrowing experiences and display endless patience if you are game to join them. They direct their short attention spans and curiosity toward varied and far-flung interests. Their inborn competitiveness makes them successful at almost anything they try; when they do fail, they consider it a "learning opportunity." They have a clear and strong capacity for loyalty, fairness, and justice. They have superior linear reasoning skills. They have the geographic sense of homing pigeons. They don't see good or bad hair; they see blond or brunette. No thigh is a fat thigh if there is any prospect they can lay their hands on it—*ever, in their lifetime.*

Boys don't "get" the talk thing in general. For them, talking is a means to an end. They need to end all conversations in some state of resolution. For girls, talking is a means to the beginning—of the next conversation. Boys can gossip, but the multilevel, mean-spirited megaduplicity perfected by girl groups is beyond their ability. Boys can be petty, but they're rarely catty. And don't be fooled if you find a boy who can gossip. Boys' gossip always has a purpose; girls' gossip is an art form. You guys have already figured out that playing with boys means getting socked or pushed; playing with girls means staying up all night talking.

Girls "work through their issues," boys plow through theirs. Boys know how to fight without holding grudges or crying, screaming, slamming doors, hanging up, or vowing indefinite separation. (Does that sound familiar?) They get over arguments in nanoseconds.

Whether or not it's remotely justified, boys are confident. Their confidence is infectious. If they experience a fleeting moment of insecurity, they're very likely to deny it, unless they're creative types who can channel it productively into the next novel, painting, or design, while girls channel their insecurity into a race through the racks at the store we like to call "Needless Markup." Everyday, normal macho men would rather date Lorena Bobbit than admit their insecurity. (Their sturdy efforts to appear so strong can be counterproductive. If you can't face your feelings, you can't fix the problem.) Girls can get lost in their insecurities. Boys are more likely to use theirs as catalysts for action: fear of failure can produce massive focus.

I don't know why boys are generally more confident than girls. It may be that they're *not* really more confident, just less conscious. This could be because girls have more connectors between their two brain spheres and, therefore, can better connect thoughts to words. If you're really interested, there are many good books on gender brain differences. There's also a ton of literature on general gender difference, and there are efforts to eradicate its possible external causes in schools, efforts like separating girls out in middle school for math and science and encouraging extracurricular activities for girls that build confidence through success. Matty just had a big confidence boost when she confronted a boy who called her stupid. The teacher gave him the r-e-s-p-e-c-t talk, and when the teacher left, Matty said to the boy, "Thank you for respecting my feelings," to which he replied, "I'm really sorry, I was just having a bad day."

Given the long relationship between this darling boy and Matty, I'm confident his original insult was the eight-year-old version of flirting. But Matty didn't feel flirted with, she felt dissed. Standing up for herself gave her the security to stand up to other, truly insensitive kids. (Sweet-natured children always attract the meanies.)

I still don't always "get" men and I never got over wanting to be able to do what boys do. And I have done most of it, but my most astounding adventures have been ones only girls can do.

Which of course, forever and always, is having my babies.

So girls, *vive la différence.*

XOXO,
Mom

RAGING HORMONES:
WHAT WAS GOD
THINKING?

Dear Hormone Handmaids,

Okay, I've heard all the horror stories. Every mom has one. If the line is long at "Tar-jhay," as we call Target (where we spend half our lives), you can strike up the conversation with total stranger moms and they'll spill their tales of woe. The gist of these is that once your daughters go into full-fledged puberty, you're at each other's throats for a while. I can't bear the idea of "losing you" for two or three years when there are so precious few to begin with. These stories shoot my primal protective forces into DEFCON 1 status. If I could ask for one mother miracle, it would be the ability to protect you from the thoroughly disorienting travails of puberty.

For the life of me, I cannot understand how the same divine or biological force that enables your body to create life can also plunge it into enough estrogen-soaked emotional chaos to make your family members remove all sharp objects from your vicinity.

I have yet to hear a positive puberty story from any fellow mother. Or even a neutral one. For mothers, puberty is an unparalleled test of unconditional love for the sweet child who has seemingly overnight morphed into a snarly, moody teen. For daughters, it is an uncontrollable journey on which you're hijacked by your body, your mom is always on your case, no one understands you, and your mirror is suddenly a funhouse reflection of greasy hair, zits, and sweaty pits.

I'm not talking here about the "birds and the bees" chat, which I'll discuss in another letter and which we've been having since you were four (in increasingly detailed and advanced versions to match your deepening curiosity). I want to talk about raging hormones, which kick in as you're starting menstruation (a hideous, totally nondescriptive word you will never use for your "friend," itself among the stupider euphemisms of all time but preferable to the many *too* descriptive words boys typically use) and grab you by the throat periodically—no pun intended—for most of your life.

When I was growing up, any sex reference, but especially menstruation, was such a taboo topic that my mom kept her Kotex sanitary napkins inside a brown paper bag behind the big bath towels on the highest shelf she could reach. When I was just learning to read, I discovered them and proudly set the table with those strange-looking but clearly absorbent "napkins." Ma didn't make a big deal of it, just lowered her voice, led me to her bedroom, and closed the door. The moment felt somehow special, just between us! She dug the rest of the concealed Kotex out of the linen closet and explained their function.

I don't remember any specific information from that lecture, but a very strong message got through. To men, this fact of life was unspeakable. Not a bad or good fact, just one that you were never, ever to allude to, even remotely, around boys or your father. To this day I cringe when any man speaks of any woman's menstrual cycle. To me it's a private and inappropriate topic between men and women. Having grown up with five sisters in a small house, Daddy isn't quite so uptight, but he has learned to stay clear of the subject with me.

While Ma made sure I was prepped on chapter and verse of the mechanics of menstruation, she didn't really tell me anything about what it would feel like or how it would affect me emotionally. So I was pretty unprepared for the first visit from "my friend."

We were on vacation. I was totally geared up for a rare week of fun and freedom. We always vacationed with my parents' circle of friends in family places where the kids could run wild on their own while the parents did whatever they did, which was mostly smoke cigarettes and tell a bunch of stories that made them all screech with laughter. I was particularly excited because my birthday fell at the beginning of our festivities, so my party would be attended by extra adults trapped into gift giving!

I'll never forget my eleventh birthday, not for the gifts or setting but for an earth-shattering event. The day after my party, I got my first visit from "my friend." I immediately told my mom, who immediately told all her girlfriends. This event created much coffee klatching among the women, who used my news bulletin as a point of departure for a particular bonding session, a reassertion of their status in their own special club. For all the secretive buildup and the women's embracing response—treating me differently, as closer to them somehow, less like a kid—I couldn't fathom what all the fuss was about.

I began to get an inkling when my mom told me I had to call off my horseback ride that afternoon. *What?* No one ever said anything about "my friend" cutting into my fun! I threw a fit. I wailed. Wept. Carried on in ways I had never before. My mom relented with the caveat, "Let's see how you feel later." That calmed me down enough to ponder my extreme, and new for me, reaction to Ma's pronouncement. I'd never felt so *emotional . . . anxious . . . different.* And then I felt *sick as a dog.*

I got clammy, fevered, nauseous, dizzy, which was nothing compared to what followed: my lower abdomen clenched up like I'd been kicked by a horse. I doubled over. And stayed that way for the remainder of our vacation.

This little adventure with "my friend" occurred like clockwork for the remainder of my teenage years. And since you weren't supposed to talk about it, I pretty much suffered in silence. I just hunkered down with a heating pad.

No one explained the onslaught of histrionics and hysteria that always preceded "my friend's" visit. No one told me that my supercramps were worse than most and I should take something. No one really talked about it at all. I am not trying to scare you. In fact, it's different now, thank God; you need to know that *nobody* suffers physically like that anymore—take two Advil, drink lots of water, and you're good to go—and *everybody* talks about their PMS now.

There are all kinds of ways to mitigate your monthly pain; I have yet to find one to put a dent in the calamitous emotional upheaval. Some girls feel flattened, others just a little bit more irritable, but I don't know anyone who doesn't feel more emotional—and more baffled by the degree to which they're likely to overreact to life's little annoyances. All those helpful magazines tell you to get more exercise and cut out coffee and alcohol. That is good advice, but let me give you a little warning: The last thing you'll want to do is get up on a StairMaster (you'll barely want to get out of bed). And you will KILL for a cup of coffee to jump-start the day and a glass of wine to unwind. Even if you run a marathon and restrict your intake to water, you'll still be teetering on the verge of tears.

Oh, did I mention bloating and zits?

The onset of menstruation marks your official start of puberty. The health books actually describe puberty as a process that begins years earlier, with the budding, etc., but I mean the milestone of getting your period for the first time. In my mind, one day I was a kid; the next, a walking cramp. That monthly menace only punctuated even greater physical and emotional upheaval. It happened so fast, it was almost impossible to keep up with the startling growth; overnight my straight, taut, manageable body swelled, stretched, rounded. I remember staring into a full-length mirror, not unpleased with the emerging curves and protuberances, but not recognizing the reflection.

But I was completely flummoxed by the equally unknown tyrant who took over my moods. One day way up, next day deep down. It was emotional whiplash by the hour, with no provocation, no rationale, no control. Once, when he made some smart-aleck crack, I heaved an entire ham across the kitchen at my boyfriend. As I matured, I looked for more responsible ways to deal with people. Like taking off in my mom's car and not stopping until I got to Nashville . . . from *Chicago!*

I have no idea what your hormonally induced mood swings will be like: anywhere from cloudy with a chance of showers to Force 10 hurricane warnings. But I do know that chances are good that once this time of life starts, you and I will be fighting about the Top Ten Teen Troublemakers: smoking, drinking, driving, peer pressure, independence, drugs, sex, eating disorders, laziness, depression. We'll talk about some of these topics in other letters. For now, just know that raging hormones are going to make it more difficult for you to summon your common sense and smarts in those dicey situations.

This is where teenage girls get into trouble—by acting too quickly on emotions evoked by the hormone roller coaster. Plus, emerging research shows teens' brains are actually changing, so some of those smart brain cells might not actually be where you left them the next time you look for them.

The only control mechanism you have is recognition. Understand that this stranger is the person you're becoming. It's critical at this time that you slow yourself down and think, *before* you act, of the *consequences* of your acts. Appreciate that hormones run amok can take normal adolescent moments of doubt and blow them up out of all proportion. The slightest offhand comment will make you feel like such a freak show, you'll vow to run away and join the circus. I promise you that within a day or even a couple of hours, you'll snap out of the mood. Don't give in to it. Distract yourself. Go to the movies, read a book, take a hot bath. Call a girlfriend. Have a good cry. Just stay away from boys feigning sympathy and sharp objects.

The weirdest phenomenon is when you get so deep into one of those unavoidable funks that you can't imagine ever feeling good again, but when the funk lifts (and it always does), you can't imagine how you could have felt so awesomely bad. Even weirder, no matter how many times you go through the cycle, how much you prepare, it always takes you over.

And here's another divine monkey wrench thrown into the works. At the very time I want to be the dispassionate sounding board for your emerging problems and concerns, I'm being inducted as an involuntary member of the Happy Hormone Club.

Menopause.

Pause.

Yes, I see you pausing here, thinking (a) Oh no, Mom is gonna tear up again (better she's crying than crabbing), and (b) Oh no, even worse, Mom is gonna hug the breath out of us and slobber all over our faces.

Well, I will concede an occasional mood shift. Okay, we can get that Dr. Jekyll–Mr. Hyde thing happening in a heartbeat.

But menopause isn't really all that bad. Just a few teeny-tiny annoyances like blinding headaches, nighttime swims in your own sweat, hot flashes that make you feel like you've just done a dozen Tabasco sauce shots, frequent loss of all brain function and/or memory, and your dad's personal favorite: moods that swing like the Flying Wallendas.

Okay, sure, it can be slightly disturbing, but to avoid

home-front turbulence, communication is key. I help Daddy be the supersupportive spouse I know he really wants to be by giving him a little heads-up. When I feel a bit "off," I just place a plaque in his bathroom: I'M OUT OF ESTROGEN AND I'VE GOT A GUN. He picks up on my subtle cue and either leaves for South America or buys me a new car.

So you see, it's not that bad.

Here's your mother's best treatment for the hormone hamster wheel: good girlfriends.

They are a fail-safe antidote. It's a scientific fact that a dose of similarly situated sisters can turn you from Charles Manson into Mother Teresa. Fellow travelers through the change of life are not only restorative and calming but productive. My friends and I are polishing some excellent comedy stand-up based on our recurring symptoms.

Like me, you have a special source of sanity: a blood sister close in age. When you see Aunt Renie and me braying hyenalike, bent over double with a hernia from laughing so hard, it's pretty likely we've been exchanging night sweat stories, a genre popular only with the initiated.

So I want you to remember a few things. When I tell you I understand what you're going through when I see your moods swinging from the chandelier, it's not just because I remember what it felt like to be a teenage girl whose body is being hijacked by hormones against her will. It's because I'm a fifty-something whose body is being

hijacked by hormones against her will *at this very moment.*
And if you don't believe me, just ask your father. So I'm
going to cut you just a teeny little bit of slack and hope
you'll do the same for me.

Raging hormones, which are no excuse for stupid, un-
kind, or dangerous actions, are actually more depressing
than debilitating. There was a time when women were
deemed incapable of holding political office just because
their monthly emotional hiatus might put them in the
mood to rip the bloody bark off anyone in their way. (Now
that's considered *mandatory* in politics!) Your job is to understand that your body is reacting this way and to slow
down and think things through even more to compensate.

You'll find your own solutions. You'll have the good
sense to dig for the information that will help you, and
most important, you'll keep a strong sense of humor.

One more thing. There *is* such a thing as male menopause. Men usually get into serious denial over it, but
whenever you see a man your father's age with a girl your
babysitter's age in a car from his teenage fantasy (convert-
ible Corvette, Mustang, etc.), be grateful that *you* can just
paste on an estrogen patch. These old geezers, in denial
over their own hormonal meltdown, are always the jerks
who utter sociopathic idiocies like "Hey, hon, is it that
time of the month?" to any woman who treats them like
the harebrains they are.

So it's not always pretty from about ages eleven to fifty-six, but it's not all ugly either. In fact, these hormones from hell are the same ones that make for so many heavenly events and experiences: they explode your compassion and passion; they jump-start your creative engine; they enhance all your senses and deepen your thought processes. They make you "feel like a natural woman"—which is the highest order of humankind God created!

XOXO,
Mom

P.S. I don't hug the breath out of you and slobber-kiss you all over because of raging hormones. I do it because you are my life.

THE VIRTUE
OF VIRTUES

Dear Vessels of Values,

You're going to think this is *the* most goober letter of all time, but it's the most important.

Someday you'll thank me. That's what my mom always said and she was right.

Parents' most critical job is to instill values in their children, to teach them how to live a virtuous life, to be a person of character. Many parents (and cultural observers) feel that teaching and living a moral life is getting beyond our capacity in today's high-tech, hyperpaced, anything goes, overexposed, materialistic, groupthink, politically correct, victimological culture.

They're wrong. We do live in a difficult day, but we're neither unique nor ill equipped to live well and right. Each generation has its ills and woes; each has to confront challenges to its values. And in turn, each generation has the familial and civic obligation to define and preserve its best and truest values.

This is always an interesting struggle in a democracy, which values individual freedom above all. Freedom spawns many and varied definitions of "true values." In open and tolerant societies, freedom can and often does mean that you're free to be an idiot. We'll talk about freedom, democracy, civic values (and political morons) in another letter. I'll just note here that the magnificence of our country didn't happen by accident. It's the cumulative result of countless acts of good citizenship carried out by innumerable individuals empowered by the gift of freedom and the impetus of powerfully held values. I believe that a country can only be as good as its individual citizens.

So while you should and, given your upbringing, likely will participate vigorously in the democratic process, before you can be a good citizen, you have to be a good person. What goes into being a good person has changed little from generation to generation, no matter what the contemporary conflicts and challenges.

Participating in the loud and heated dialogue of democracy over cultural values is no replacement for the solitary acquisition of universal, time-honored, personal values. Culture wars can be trendy; the edicts passed down by the winners of the latest hot-button debate are as long-standing as those decreed by the arbiters of *Vogue*. The real values you'll work to acquire won't change no matter which way the cultural winds blow.

You girls are already displaying a deep curiosity about what's right and wrong, what's true and real for yourselves and your surroundings. Your endless questions range from truly advanced ("If you are antiabortion, you're anti–death penalty, right? That goes together, right?") to extremely annoying ("Why won't you let me pray for Osama?"), but I'm always moved by your innocent, guileless quest for a value system. You demand to know everything from why some men are more evil than the devil (whom you curiously do not believe in) to how you can be "good"; what does "good" mean? Will your being good make me and Daddy happy?

I'm always at a loss to explain to you the unspeakable evil, barbarity, and cruelty of the maniacs who color your developing worldview today. But I do have a few pointers on being good (besides shouting at you for being bad!) that carry over from my mom's time.

Achieving and living a balanced, rich, moral, fulfilling, productive life of character is a tricky business. Ma had clear guidelines. She had a long litany of Ben Franklinisms on various virtues, but she had only two basic guiding principles, loosely derived from the Bible, from which all else flowed:

1. Do unto others as you would have them do unto you.
2. Be true to yourself.

By her reckoning and my experience, these are two sides of the same coin and mutually reinforcing. In order to treat others the way you want to be treated, you need to know who you are and stay true to that. I can explain values and teach you many virtues, but only you can find your unique selves.

Ma wasn't especially religious. Or at least she didn't talk openly about her faith. She had a deep, quiet faith manifested in a single saying, "There are no atheists in foxholes." We'll talk about faith and religion in a separate letter, but whether or not you become a practicing person of faith, you can learn most anything you need to know about living a good life by studying the life of Jesus.

The story of Jesus and his disciples will give you incomparable guidance on the glory of staying true to yourself, as Mary Magdalene did. (You will also learn about the painful consequences of losing faith in yourself, as Judas did.) And you will see the awesome compelling power of the Golden Rule—a power that literally transforms individuals, cultures, and indeed, the world.

You've been baptized in the Roman Catholic Church and you attend an Episcopalian school. But other world religions have much to offer on values and history and culture. We have many Jewish friends, and your father and I are staunch supporters of Israel (but that has as much to do with politics as religion). Your Aunt Renie has done a lot of study of Eastern religions. While you're growing up, we're all getting a crash course on Islam. You should study it all; the values I'm talking about here are universal, and you'll find them in every religion you study.

Whenever we had one of our many mother-daughter talks about life, Ma would always start with "Do unto others as you would have them do unto you" or "Be true to yourself" or both. Then she'd get another cup of coffee, light up yet another ciggie, and exhale other iterations of her basic rules: "Love your neighbor as you love yourself," "You need to walk a mile in her moccasins," or "You can't hide from yourself."

She usually avoided the particulars of our many daily issues (except those concerning boys, a topic she dissected in every detail). She prodded us kids to try to figure out answers for ourselves, guided by those clear-cut basics. She was right; if you start there, you can always find your way home. So go there first to get grounded.

Virtues are the building blocks of character; they're how you live out your basic value system. You've already heard so much about the virtues Daddy and I treasure: perseverance, respect, empathy, responsibility, fairness, humility, courage, forgiveness. However, the virtue we prize above all and the one that will serve you best is honesty.

The two tenets of Ma's basic value system are wholly erected on honesty. Consider the first principle: Do unto others as you would have them do unto you. Is there anything worse than being lied to? You must always tell the truth; you must always fulfill your commitments; your word must be your bond.

Daddy has a stained glass window in his den that was designed by Frank Lloyd Wright, an architect who once said, "The truth is more important than the facts." Every time you watch TV with Daddy, I want you to look at the Wright window and think about that. Every day you hear the same thing: the worst thing you can do is lie. I pound this into you every day, not to "hear myself talk" (another momism), but because liars are losers.

Now I have to be honest, just to prepare you: sadly, not all liars lose. And just to confuse you, not all lies are equal. Daddy likes to say, "There's the truth, the whole truth, and nothing but the truth. Which one do you want?" You don't always have to tell *nothing* but the truth. For instance, here are a few of the nothing-but-the-truths you've shared with me when silence would have been golden: "Your new haircut is awful," "That lipstick is too red," "You're the oldest mother in class," and my personal favorite, "You have a squishy butt."

These kinds of "truth" are forbidden by a universal momism: If you can't say something nice, keep your pie-hole buttoned up. Even when someone asks you a direct question, like "Do I look fat in this?"

People who have an irrepressible need to be compulsively critical (like some of the mean girls in your classes) grow up to be professional critics. Professional critics are mostly people too insecure or lazy to commit themselves to real action, so they carp from the sidelines. They deserve neither your respect nor attention. Being honest doesn't require telling hurtful truths to make yourself feel superior.

An insidious, pervasive form of dishonesty is hypocrisy. You'll meet many hypocrites who talk the talk but don't walk the walk. Daddy is amused by hypocrisy; it sickens me. I try hard to avoid hypocrites, harder to avoid being one. That's not easy and I'm not always successful. You should call me on it if you see it. In fact, you already do; when I'm nice to someone you overheard me gossiping about, my punishment is that you always tell the gossipee what I said!

By definition, Ma's second guiding principle—Be true to yourself—is based solely on honesty. You may often be tempted by peers or fads (which parade as "progress") to behave in ways or believe in things that don't jibe with your own value system. You may even try to *deny* your own principles to fit in or get ahead. You will never be successful, or happy, being anyone but yourself. Lying to yourself may be even worse than lying to others. More wisdom from the Bible: "Ye shall know the truth, and the truth shall make you free." (John 8:32) Self-deception is enslavement. Self-deception is sneaky. It slowly oozes in, roots, and chokes you off from yourself. When you're lost from yourself, you'll feel stuck, one-dimensional. At the first sign of frustration, boredom, or free-floating anger, conduct a self-examination. You'll know you're being dishonest with yourself if the first thing you do is deny it. Then you'll wince and twist. When you finally get it into focus, face your problem. If you face it, you can fix it. If you don't deal with your daily issues, they'll turn into lifelong demons. And if you don't listen to your own conscience, you'll become a demon! Ma was right; you can't hide from yourself.

To stay true to yourself you have to keep a steady fix on *who you are*. Check in with yourself often, even without emotional prompting. Take time to reassess your values; ask yourself if you're living up to your own standards. This doesn't mean an endless quest for "self-actualization" or whatever the current euphemism is for self-absorption. Frank introspection is good; navel-gazing is not.

Maybe we just have too much leisure time, so we waste it on "finding ourselves" instead of strengthening our character. Our parents' generation had neither the time nor, as far as I could tell, the inclination to get all twisted up seeking personal fulfillment; they couldn't care less about locating their inner child. When I (finally, after seven years of almost as many majors) graduated from college and moved back in with my parents, I informed them that I needed a job that would be emotionally fulfilling. They informed me that I needed a job that would fill my stomach. These were people who went to bed hungry as kids. Their idea of personal fulfillment was being able to provide for their families.

I listened to countless conversations my mom had with her girlfriends—on the phone, in her beauty shop, on the front porch, coffee-klatching—and I never once heard her or any of them talk about their "inner child" or "self-actualization." She and her friends were obsessed with their real children who had real needs. These were the most amazingly "self-actualized" women I knew: smart, strong, resourceful. My mom didn't give me a how-to book on finding myself. She made me figure it out for myself like she did.

And I will confess to many a pointless quest in search of self. You'll doubtless go on many pointless quests yourselves—I wouldn't want you to miss them in a million years, because you'll learn so much from getting them wrong—but let me offer you one surefire shortcut: if it doesn't feel right, it probably isn't. If you're working overtime to convince yourself something is good, it's probably bad. But not so fast; the converse of this rule—if it feels good, do it—is *not* true. If it feels good and you want to do it, first ask yourself a few questions: Is it immoral, unlawful, or dangerous? (Aunt Pat's test) What would be the present and future consequences for you of doing it? (our longtime friend Jon Macks's test) Would it hurt or embarrass another person? (my test) Would it cost a lot of money? (Daddy's test!) And if you're still stuck, ask yourself, Would you approve of your parents' doing it? (You have very strict protocol for parental behavior! You really keep us on the straight and narrow!)

I don't mean this to sound like a sermon, or harder than it is. We live in a country built on values; you are surrounded by people who work in professions that promote values; you go to a loving school with a value-based curriculum. Your friends come from families who share our values.

My mother used to sum all that up with a working-class European saying, "You come from good stock." I just want to encourage you to reflect on your values, to understand that goodness is neither a given nor an accident. The values of great countries, communities, families, and people are universal and timeless. You were born of this system and have a responsibility to pass it on.

You already make me so proud with the values you display even at such a young age. We'll keep working on our character—all of us together. But if you're ever stuck somewhere, sometime, without me, know that the values my mom anchored in me are anchored in you and you will never be lost.

And you will always be loved.

XOXO,
Mom

Boys: The AP Course

Dear Girls,

I was going to call this letter "Boys, Part Deux: Sex Machines Run Amok," but I was afraid that might be tipping my hand too soon. But get real. It's time for your mother to inform you of the single, overarching, primary, even primal—*listen to me now*—difference between girls and boys and the absolutely critical thing to understand about boys: the center of their universe, the core of their being, their 24-7, their raison d'être, their Holy Grail, the very essence of life for them is sex. Or as Matty says, "s-e-x." Matty, when you and I reviewed the topics for these letters, you asked if we could substitute the topic of s-e-x for politics. Then you thought better of it and, ever one to avoid confrontation, you concluded we should leave out both topics!

But we need to get down to the nitty-gritty of the sex

talk, the next in our series of "birds and bees" conversations. You are exposed to so much, so early. You ask me questions at your age that I didn't think of till high school. I remember with amazing clarity my confusion when our fifth-grade teacher kicked all the boys out of the classroom and papered over our windows to ensure the privacy of our ensuing instruction. Which was an eight-millimeter herky-jerky film on how a baby is made. Not only was I clueless relative to the subject matter, I was incredulous over the boys' departure. When the incomprehensible film ended, our teacher said, "If you have any questions, ask your mothers."

So I did. Ma was very matter-of-fact about the basics but supcranimated about the complex philosophy of sex, which she had reduced to a mantra she urged on me almost every day from age ten on through high school: "Boys would screw a snake if it would lay still long enough." She had various iterations on this theme, which she felt inspired to repeat to me and my girlfriends every time we said the word *boys*. For example, "No matter what they say, they won't respect you," or "Why buy the cow when you can get the milk for free?" or "They play, you pay. Boys don't have babies."

Let's flash forward forty years and allow your mother to give you a twenty-first-century take on boys and s-e-x. Boys would screw a snake if it would lay still long enough. (A lot of men think that's a compliment.) And today we have to consider a whole new and dangerous array of the more likely consequences of early sex, like STDs, date rape, abortion, and the emotional chaos caused by sex in immature relationships.

There is no point trying to dissuade your boyfriends of their obsession with sex. You may even get dumped for refusing to have sex; I did. It broke my heart but not my resolve. Do not get angry. Do not take it personally. *It is not about you.* You are no match for the survival gene. Males were put on this earth to make progeny—as many as possible. The female yang to this yin is to protect and rear to child-producing age those progeny; the fewer a woman has, the more likely she is to succeed. In other words, men and women are biologically hardwired to have opposite goals. I never got this rudimentary reality until I started reading feminist literature in the 1970s. If I'd understood it earlier, I could have spared myself a lot of angst, confusion, heartbreak, and outrage.

Here's something you may not hear often enough in a world where we're all so terrified that our children will get pregnant by mistake, contract an STD, or have their hearts or lives trashed by a horrible sexual experience. Sex is a beautiful thing. A magical, breathtaking, blinding, unparalleled experience. Also just plain fun, if, if, if—*are you listening?*—you engage with a man you love in a mature, trusting, secure relationship.

I realize this is ostensibly archaic thinking. Everything

you see on television, in magazines, and at the movies or hear from your friends belies this sentiment. We live in an age of buddy sex and we-shared-a-latte-so-let's-have-sex and oral-sex-isn't-really-sex. You're just going to have to trust your mother on this. This age-old advice is still true, will always be true, and oral sex most certainly counts. You two are going to have to deal early and often with the stress of sex. You're already beautiful girls and you're going to be stunning teens. You have compelling features and great little figures. My mother rarely swore, and never in anger, but she did have a few colorful choice phrases. One of my all-time favorites was "She's built like a brick shit house," which is going to describe both of you. That package is called a boy magnet. Let me remind you to not be (overly) flattered by boys' attentions, as they will say anything, etc., etc., etc.!

Even more problematic are your individual natures. Matty, you are sweet and empathetic. You tend to feel sorry for almost everyone who even looks like they might be having a bad day. You will do anything to brighten the way. That great virtue will make you walking prey. Emma, you are daring and adventurous and contrary. Those great attributes will paint a big fat boy bull's-eye on your back.

On the other hand, you both have that delightful quality of "It's my way or the highway!" (Where did you get that?) Which is a good foundation for dealing with testosterone-overloaded young bucks. More than anything else in your entire life, when it comes to sex, *you are in control.* Only you can say yes. Only you hold the ultimate promise. This is a very potent power. Controlling this power means controlling yourself.

The key to controlling yourself in the face of his pressure and your desire is to remember first and foremost to consider the consequences, short- and long-term, of intimate relations. There are *always* consequences. Let's start with the emotional issues and damage to reputation. Whether you like it or not, there's no such thing as "casual sex," at least not for girls.

The centerpiece of the last female liberation movement was the idea that girls can do anything boys can do— including, and maybe especially, dumb and cheap and selfish things, like casual, meaningless sex. This was one of the many myths of "equal rights." It took about twenty or thirty years for girls to discover there was a big reason boys were buying into women's lib with such gusto: they got easy lays. Well, there's nothing easy about it for girls. All my mom's rules apply—especially, "They play, you pay."

Liberated women in their thirties started looking around for stability, commitment, a return on their investment. And guess what they learned? "Why buy the cow when you can get the milk for free?"

Girls are returning to some version of the old-fashioned expectation that their relationships have significance and romance. Girls *demand* respect today. When I was a teen, I had a lot of friends who were boys, and I was appalled at the way they repeated every (usually exaggerated) intimate detail of every minute of any encounter with any girl.

There was a clique of girls who "did it"; the boys would circle and sniff around them like starving wolves. As soon as they got "fed," they would drop the girl and trash her. Even with their own special girlfriends, these guys made sure all their boy friends knew they were "getting it." To this day, I hear men gossip about professional women "sleeping around." I'm talking single, mature, independent women. This, my dears, is called the double standard. It starts in middle school and *never stops.*

As disconcerting as the emotional chaos caused by sex can be, it can't hold a candle to the health issues involved with unthinking sex.

I know you're going to hear about all this in your health class, but I'm not trusting to anyone else anything as important as imparting this information, and I want you to hear it from someone who loves you and treasures your health and well-being. STDs can cause lifelong problems, including infertility. HIV and AIDS can cause death. Birth control pills don't protect against these ravages. The heartbreaking consequence is unwanted pregnancy.

You have the power to make your own decisions. It is *your* choice to have sex, and no one can make you get pregnant. If you get pregnant by mistake, you're the one who ultimately has to deal with the consequences. Not the baby's father. You. No one who isn't willing to grapple with the grim realities of every one of those scenarios has any business having sex.

Obviously, you do not have control over sex forced on you. If any man ever attacks you, I swear to God, I will kill him. I will not be governed by the law of man because those men are beasts. I can't bear to think, let alone write about such unspeakable acts, but know this. When those horrible, despicable things happen, they are *never* the girl's fault.

Okay, so let's get back to how to avoid *having* to deal with unwanted pregnancy, STDs, HIV, and all the rest.

Understanding all the consequences, as dire as they are, may not be enough motivation for you to practice total self-control. You can actually get truly crazy and overwhelmed in an overheated situation, even when you don't intend to. The best way to avoid an unexpected blast furnace where you might not be able to control yourself is to control your environment. Don't put yourself in hard-to-control situations with boys, or at parties, or with too much drinking or fast friends.

You won't be able to avoid every potential sex situation, because boys make every situation one with the potential for sex. If you find yourself inadvertently in a compromising position, the time-honored tactic is—and yes, you can do it—*just say no!*

They may whine, they may actually break down and cry, they will certainly beg, but the ones worth your time won't think badly of you for calling the shots. In fact they'll respect you for respecting yourself. For taking control of the situation and keeping yourself under control. If they don't, screw 'em (no pun intended).

So you're in the driver's seat. Don't employ your power for insincere purposes, i.e., teasing boys. Flirting is a fine art; coming on is sadistic, not to mention *scary*. The law now says a boy must stop any time a girl tells him to, no matter how much she's "come on," but there's the law of man and the laws of nature. You might win in court, but it's close to impossible to beat back nature.

These are some rough topics, but it's my responsibility to cover them and your responsibility to think hard about them. Let's get back to normal sex—actually, there's no such thing—I mean, healthy sex.

My own mother was far more permissive than I will be, probably because she had been a better kid than I was and couldn't imagine the scary stunts I pulled. My being me is why I worry so much about you. But for all my stunts, Ma never had to worry that I'd get into trouble with sex because her life lessons on sex were very effective when I was a teen. She had a powerful partner—the fear of God! Also, the real promise that my dad would murder the boy. But she taught me best by talking, a lot, and more than anything, by giving me the certain knowledge that she would love me no matter what, so I always knew I could confide in her. I will never not be "available" when you need me. There is nothing I won't understand. You can tell me anything. You need to get out of your heads a notion that is already taking root: that I came into life as a fully formed adult. I actually was a teenager once; sure, it was a long time ago, but you never forget those first experiences and emotions. I trust you, I will never invade your privacy (too much), but we will talk.

If for some inexplicable reason you cannot or don't want to talk to me, promise me you will confide in some responsible adult. Aunt Renie or Maria or a teacher or counselor, a friend's mother. (I wouldn't talk to Daddy. He's already picked out convents for each of you.) I hope you won't ever feel you can't come to me, but please, please, please, don't close down when you feel confused.

My plan is to give you some space. I won't spy or pry, but from a distance, I'll be keeping track of you like a rat on a Cheeto. I'm going to be your control partner. I'm going to help you. I trust you and will unless you give me cause not to, but I'm going to know where you are and who you're with. We're going to talk about sex and love and relationships until the topic is tattooed on your brain. My plan, which Daddy shares, is that since there is no way to protect you from our sex-saturated culture, we will constantly infuse your exposures with moral moments. We'll try to put what you're seeing, hearing, learning prematurely into perspective, giving it a context that reflects our value system.

I realize this letter sounds harsh and prudish, scary even. And having sex irresponsibly *is* scary. But clearly, sex itself is not irresponsible, people are. Sex is extraordinary. It is the ultimate expression of love, of bonding and sharing. Procreation is nothing less than a bona fide miracle. Responsible sex is not just about avoiding ugly consequences. It's about receiving a great gift.

There's an enormous reward for waiting until you're ready with the right man: a true experience.

You girls know love, and you are so loving, you deserve nothing but the best and truest. At some point, that's out of my control. I pray I can teach you some things about avoiding mistakes, but it's totally and only in your control to make miracles.

XOXO,
Mom

CHARACTER
DEVELOPMENT

Dear Girls,

My dad has always lived by the maxim "Character is destiny." If you have a good, strong character, it doesn't matter how many times life knocks you down; you'll get up again. Not only will you keep on moving, you'll be better for the experience. Poppy looked for opportunities to foster character in every situation that required out-of-the-ordinary effort or carried the potential for disaster. The harder the effort or the worse the outcome, the greater the potential he saw for "character development." From the earliest age, everything we kids hated doing (cleaning the house) or failed at (flute, banjo, saxophone) became a lesson in character development. Major disappointments (like being drop-kicked by boyfriends) were the advanced placement courses on character development. To this day, it's a running joke with my sister, brother, and me. Long gas lines? Character development! Starbucks closed? Character development! Still, as we confront the real, unavoidable, sometimes painful challenges of every day, we truly do comfort ourselves that at least we're racking up character development bonus points for those losses, disappointments, and failures.

As people who have spent so much of our time involved in political campaigns, Daddy and I have lived by a corollary of character development, which is "Whatever doesn't kill you makes you stronger." Campaigns are all about confronting lapses and overcoming losses. When the odds are fifty-fifty that you're going to lose in any and all contests, you'd better be prepared to deal with failure. You can't win campaigns if you're afraid to lose.

Character that is untested by adversity or that crumbles in the face of it is unformed and weak. You'll always be able to count on character formed and forged by confronting failures, disappointments, and seemingly insurmountable problems.

Last year our whole family got an extreme test in character development and witnessed an ultimate example of character. On Labor Day weekend, my little brother, your uncle Stevie, was riding his dirt bike in a field behind his house with his buddies and his seven-year-old son. He was going about five miles an hour, wearing all his safety gear. He was heading up a small hill when his head snapped back and he suddenly dropped like a rag doll. Although his body had crumpled up in a heap and his friends were shouting and screaming for help, Stevie felt utterly removed from the turmoil. He was in a totally quiet, completely peaceful place blooming with radiant white light. When he came to consciousness, he was completely paralyzed from the neck down, able to move only his eyes. His breathing was labored and erratic.

He was medevaced to Chicago, taped to a board for two days, and given so many MRIs, CAT scans, and X-rays, we thought he would glow in the dark. He was in the neurospinal ICU for a week. The diagnosis was central cord syndrome: nothing was broken or severed, but his spinal cord had suffered extreme compression. The doctor explained that it had been smooshed like a garden hose under a truck tire. We all held our breath through the first operation, where they opened up his spinal column from the C3 to C7 vertebrae, widening his column by inserting and fusing in bones from cadavers. Stevie begged for bones from Sue the Dinosaur, on exhibit at the nearby Natural History museum. He kept trying to make us forget his prognosis. It was touch and go whether he'd emerge from surgery completely paralyzed, if he survived at all.

Then the surgeons bolted a "halo" on him—twelve pounds of devilish metal designed to keep his head completely immobile while his spine healed—with three-inch bolts they screwed through four holes they drilled directly into his skull. It was a horrifying time. Totally immobilized, his cranium trussed up like Frankenstein, he felt like God had played a dirty trick on him. He'd begun to feel some vague sensation in his hands and feet, as though he were wearing oven mitts, but he could feel any and all pain—deeply and exquisitely. He'd lost all proprioception—the ability to feel where his limbs were—and he suffered debilitating panic attacks, unable to look around to get his bearings. He was frequently terrified because he felt like his lungs were collapsing and he'd have to struggle for air.

By mid-September he could move his feet and legs a little bit and squeeze his left hand, so he was moved into a rehab center. We had no idea how long he'd be there, or what kind of progress he might make. Would he be a quadriplegic for the rest of this life?

No doctor could tell us what was coming next; no one was willing to make any predictions. The worst was the anxiety over not knowing. I don't know that I would have that strength, but Stevie, a single father, would think of his daughter and son and just keep pushing himself. Every day, he made progress, but it came in such stingy increments that we all wanted to weep. The bathroom issues were the ultimate indignity, but Stevie declared an "anti-pity potty party" and just kept chanting his mantra, "Character development Character development. Character development." Only once, after yet another day of pain and frustration, did I hear him say, "I don't know how much more character I can develop."

Stevie's like me: a total control freak. He never asks us for anything, so it was awful for him to have to depend on us for every little thing. But he never lost his sense of humor. When the occupational therapist encouraged him to set a goal for his therapy, Stevie didn't hesitate: "I want to be able to pick my own nose." We all laughed hysterically. The day he was able to reach up and scratch his own nose—hallelujah! Renie sent the e-mail heard 'round the world: Stevie can pick his own nose! That sense of humor got us all through.

He couldn't bear to have us feeling sorry for him. One day he told Jim, Renie's husband, that he was "just too tired" to go to the bathroom—a grueling forty-five-minute ordeal. Then he stopped himself and said, "No, that sounds too much like a quitter."

Renie and Jim spent the most time with Stevie, but I was with him the day he took his first step, four weeks after the accident. It was an ordeal just to sit him up in his wheelchair, his head bolted inside that heavy halo. (Stevie had already agreed to wire it with Christmas lights if he was still wearing it in December.) Slowly the therapist and I pulled him up to standing and helped him steady himself with his arms on a walker. It took such tremendous effort to balance that Frankenstein head, while being unable to feel where his legs were, that he actually turned greenish gray. He was terrified, sweating, gasping for breath, struggling to find any balance. He stood for a few seconds, then

collapsed back into the chair, utterly drained. The therapist said, "Okay, that's enough." He said, "No, it isn't." "No,
Stevie," I begged. "It's enough." But he insisted. He made
us pull him back up again. He stood there with his eyes
squeezed shut with concentration, gritting his teeth, and
then he proceeded to take a step, not even knowing where
his foot was. He kept walking for ten steps, tears streaming
down his face from the pain. The therapist begged him to
stop: "That's enough, Steve." But he just kept going, each
step more painful than the last. He wouldn't even look at
me, because he knew I was crying. He just said, "Shut up.
Don't even think about it."

Stevie never stopped trying to find the palest trace of a
silver lining in this huge black thundercloud. One day he
announced to the nurse, "Hey, I quit smoking!"

"Terrific!" she cheered. "When did you do that?"

"The day of my accident."

One afternoon I kidnapped Stevie from the rehab center for a little adventure. He was dressed in the height of
hospital chic, with his Frankenstein halo, a hospital john-
ny, and a pair of sweatpants. I rolled his wheelchair up and
down Michigan Avenue; he kept making me turn the chair
so he could feel the sun on his face. Determined to have
real Starbucks coffee, he had me link three straws together
so he'd be able to sip it himself, without my hovering. As
we paused at a street corner, waiting for the light to
change, a huge city bus pulled up, drowning us in exhaust

fumes. Stevie just took a deep breath, as though he were taking a drag on a Marlboro, had another sip of his latte, beamed his thousand-watt smile, and pronounced, "Ah, this is the life!"

Through the worst of this ordeal, I saw the best in the people around me. People of character attract folks with similar values. Steve's best friends, Dale and Pam, without hesitation took in his teenage daughter and brand-new puppy for weeks; his buddies from work looked out for him so he could keep some kind of income. Uncle Jim took weeks of leave time from his Head Start job to sit at Steve's bedside and massage his atrophying arms and legs. Aunt Renie organized all our schedules, moving us back and forth from DC to Chicago, despite having just started a new job in her beloved field. She's a teacher specializing in working with children with learning disabilities, and she'd waited quite a while for the perfect teaching opportunity. Finally, it had come along—exactly the students she most wanted to work with, the ideal commute, a decent salary. But the minute she realized that Stevie was in a bad jam, she quit that perfect job without a backward glance. Now that's character!

Seven weeks after the accident, Stevie went home. By now he could feed and dress himself, but everything would be a struggle. It would take an hour and a half to get dressed, and then he'd be exhausted. His son, little Stevie, saw that he was having trouble, so he just climbed up on the bed to help him button his pants. Stevie couldn't lift anything heavier than four pounds; a gallon of milk is eight pounds. He'd get so discouraged because everything he'd taken for granted was just so hard. He could manage a trip out to the mailbox, but still unable to feel exactly where his legs were, he looked like the Minister of Silly Walks. More than anything, though, he wanted his kids to see that he'd never give up.

Stevie recently visited the doctor, four months out from the accident. The doctor looked him over and said, "You need to be thankful for what God has given you back. I never expected to see you out of a wheelchair. I thought you'd be catheterized for the rest of your life." That was the first time Stevie heard such a dire prognosis. He just swallowed hard and said, "I am thankful, but it's not enough. This is not acceptable." He's not satisfied with forty percent. He is in constant pain and no one even now has any idea how much he can recover, but he *believes* his recovery is in his hands, and he's not gonna quit.

Stevie is by nature a modest guy; he doesn't like drawing attention to himself. Yet when I asked him, "Can I use your story to explain character development?" he said, "If you think telling this story will help somebody else, then I'm okay with it. If out of all this, some good can come, then go ahead." He's allowed me to share these painful, private moments because he hopes that sharing his struggles will inspire someone else to work through their challenges. I don't know a finer example of character.

I pray you won't be tested the way Uncle Stevie's been tested, or for that matter, the way your cousin Celena, who's only fifteen, is being tested as the "woman of the house." You don't need a monumental life challenge like Stevie's to develop character; it's how you rise to the little everyday roadblocks that count. Once you've forged that character, you'll always be able to count on it to meet the big challenges. And if ever you have a moment of doubt about yourself or your abilities, close your eyes and feel Uncle Stevie hugging you—and know that you have that courage.

The threshold test of character is facing adversity with courage. Stevie has given us an unparalleled example of uncommon courage in the face of catastrophic misfortune. An absolute, necessary component of courage is conviction. Stevie believes in himself; he has confidence in his family and friends; he holds as an article of faith that his hard work and all their prayers will help him recover.

I suppose you could be courageous without any convictions, but that would be like piloting a sailboat without wind. What would be the point of undirected courage? Developing your character means developing your core beliefs and sticking to them. Character means you have to have convictions and you must be willing to fight for them.

Character is who you are and how you live day after day. It will save you from going over the edge and it will push you over the top. You can count on yourself, and just as important, others can count on you. There are no short cuts to developing character. No one can *give* you character, but if you have it, no one can take it away.

When I was your age, I never understood what Poppy or *my* dad meant when he said, "Character is destiny." I now see clearly and daily the power and promise of character.

I cannot tell you your destiny—what life holds for you. But if you are a person of character, I can assure you, you are going to hold up in life and that means *all* is possible.

> To destiny and beyond,
> Mom

GETTING YOUR
YA-YAS OUT

Dear Growing Girls,

If you remember nothing else of your childhood, you will never live long enough to forget this daily conversation that takes place about, oh, *five hundred thousand times.*

Mom: Don't do that.
Kid: Why?
Mom: Because I said so.
Kid: (Friend) does it.
Mom: You're not (friend).
Kid: (Friend's) mom lets her do it.
Mom: So, I'm not (friend's) mom.

This is the exact dialogue my mom and I had every day, well into my teens. This is a variation on a theme that *every* mom says to *every* kid *every* day. I'm positive Cave Mom told Cave Kid *don't* touch that fire, *don't* pet that saber-toothed tiger, that spear is *not a toy*.

In its early stages, this mom-kid conversation literally protected you from hurting yourself. Though this protectiveness sounds pretty mindless, there really is a skill to it. I went overboard with firstborn Matty. I once rushed you to the emergency room when you were stung by a bee. I had Daddy call one of the nation's leading pediatricians when you rolled off the couch at six months.

By the time Emma came along, I had dialed down my mom response alarm. Once she grabbed the three dogs' leashes when she was already teetering at the top of the stairs and did a triple somersault all the way down the whole flight, landing on her head. I looked down from the landing, said, "Are you okay?" and went about my business. Just kidding. I was more reactive than that; I yelled at her for leashing the dogs in the house!

Just kidding again. Emma, lest you sue me for repressed emotional damage when you're twenty-eight, I did untangle you from the dogs, leashes, table, vase, and flowers you hit at the foot of the stairs, hold, rock, and comfort you. But neither I nor you freaked out.

To this day Matty is ultracautious and Emma is especially fearless. I'm always nagging, "Matty, lighten up. Emma, rein it in." Now my job is to groom your natural cautiousness into prudence and your inborn fearlessness into adventurousness. Matty, if you end up with agoraphobia, and Emma, if you end up in jail, well, I did my best!

Grooming you means that you'll be hearing ever more sophisticated versions of "Because I said so" until you leave home and that these versions will serve an ever-changing and increasingly complex purpose. I'll be a little less concerned about your physical safety (although I'm already in high freak mode just thinking about your drivers' licenses) and zero in on preparing you for harmonious passage through life.

Being your physical safety net was pretty straightforward. When you were in danger, I acted without thinking. But the task of preparing you for life outside the family cocoon sometimes paralyzes me—and Daddy too. As we're watching you grow into your own little personalities, sometimes we feel like we have zero control. You're already saying and doing things way out of our universe. Though we can feel like passengers, we know we're still in the driver's seat, at least for a few more years.

Just as I did when I was pregnant, I've read way too many books on the topic. Some books say you'll be taking direction from us until you're five, at which point all bets are off. This I don't believe, since you're both older and clearly we still have a lot of influence over you. Other books say you'll listen to us until you're eleven or thirteen. Still other books say it's your environment, not your age, that determines whether we'll have any say over your lives. This theory makes me a little nervous, since our environment is predictably unpredictable. As I've hacked my way through all the contradictory and overwrought advice, the one certain truth that comes out of all those books is this: the best parenting is a good example.

This really freaks me out.

I lived a long time not having to be an example and pulled more than a few stunts I hope you never discover. Not being responsible for anyone except oneself can lead to some serious irresponsibility. And let's not even begin on Daddy's colorful (to put it mildly) past. Lest you think your parents were Unabombers or drug dealers, let me assure you that our careless activities were neither immoral nor unlawful, but they were sometimes stupidly dangerous. We prefer to remember them as aggressively adventurous.

Okay, I did spend a *few moments* in jail—once for protesting; once for playing too hard with my very cool brother when he was in a rock 'n' roll band. (Girls don't have the same not-getting-caught skills boys do.) As for Daddy, you couldn't replicate his adventures, inasmuch as they are peculiar to the male species.

The good news is we both surely did get our ya-ya's out. You're not going to have parents showing up at your school events dressing and acting like adolescents. We are grown-ups now. We might both be rightly accused of occasional arrested development, but we are pathologically obsessed parents. We try so hard to set a good example for you that we often laugh at ourselves. Or at least I laugh at Daddy's unconscious Ward Cleaver routine: "Girls, let's all sit down and have a nice family chat." He remains undeterred from his perfect dad routine even though you always respond the same way: "Dad, *get a life!*" (Strangely, he finds my June Cleaver becoming, but that's another letter.)

I wish I could say that sooner or later we all grow up, but it just isn't true. Many people simply become older big babies. Don't confuse growing older with growing up. You just hang out for the former but you have to work really hard for the latter. It takes more than your parents' setting and your following a good example. We'll have long talks about virtues and character, but you need a couple of clear guidelines to grow up happy and healthy and good.

It won't be long before "Don't do that, because I said so and I'm your mother" just isn't going to cut it anymore. When I'm searching for the best parenting advice to cover that more uncertain terrain, it comes as I'm falling asleep, when suddenly I'll remember what my mother said, did, or forewarned me about regarding raising kids. (Even though I told her I would never have kids right up to the end, she always knew better. Mothers know all about their kids' souls.) My dad has been a lifelong teacher of "good values" and continues to be a steady source of guidance and strength, but Ma was the keeper of the dos and don'ts list. I listened less to the don'ts but the dos stuck with me. You also roll your eyes at any sentence that begins with "Don't," so let's focus on the dos. Here's the deal. The time will come when you're gonna want to get your ya-yas out, just like Daddy and I did. And we won't be there to insist you make smart choices in tough situations; you'll be on your own. When you get there, pull out your mental do list. It's short, simple, and foolproof:

Do respect your mind. It knows right from wrong, no matter what friends or boyfriends say. Listen to it.

Do respect your heart. It's made for intimacy, which means it's made to be broken. Make sure that anyone you let in is worthy of the gift of your love.

Do respect your body; you're leasing it for the next hundred years or so. Anything you puff or pour into it affects it, and you'll never know for how long.

Do trust your parents. We get it; we've been there. I don't care if you've broken every rule in the book—snuck out of your room, shimmied down the drainpipe, driven with a fake ID and without your license to an all-night kegger. If you call us at 3 AM and ask to be picked up because you don't want to drive drunk or ride with someone who's drunk, know that we'll come get you right away, and the only consequence will be that we'll thank you for making a smart choice after a whole bunch of stupid ones.

The hardest thing for parents is knowing that in the end, we can't protect you from screwing up; we all get that education the hard way. Do know that you're going to make mistakes; do trust that there's nothing you can do that we can't get through together.

XOXO,
Mom

F R E A K - O U T

Dear Unfortunate Carriers of the Matalin DNA,

One night Daddy was telling me what a great idea these letters were and what a wonderful keepsake for you guys they will be and how he was looking forward to it and—I cut him off.

"Shut up! You're freaking me out. I can't do this!" (I was already more than half done.)

Ignoring my interruption (you really can't shut Daddy up), but taking my point, he offered a suggestion: "Why don't you talk to the children about insecurity? You're an expert at it!" (That's what's known as a backhanded compliment.)

"Gosh, thanks, honey! What the heck does *that* mean?" I responded.

Daddy shot back a classic Carvillianism: "You're the most insecure secure person I know." He can't get over how I always angst over every project, "which is stupid, just stupid, because everything you do is just the best."

"I don't really think I could do the subject justice," I fretted.

"Lord have mercy, yes you can. It'll be easy as a hot knife through butter!" Daddy replied.

Easy for him to say. My observation has been that boys presume success; girls presume disaster. Is built-in insecurity a gender thing? Is my worldview skewed by my own insecurities? In any case, building self-confidence and learning to tamp down normal insecurities is part of growing up. Your daddy reminded me what a large role your parents play in helping you do this.

Even though I cannot stop myself from trying to stave off any scary or lonely event from your young lives, I want you to know that being scared and feeling lonely are pretty normal, everyday occurrences.

Now here's some good news; fear and loneliness don't have to be forces of darkness; they can be, if you face them, extraordinarily illuminating and they can precipitate positive actions. In truth, I usually perform best when I'm scared out of my wits. And I'm often very content to be alone.

One of the ways I try to instill confidence and inoculate you against the feelings of insecurity is to overcompliment, promote, encourage, and adore every single thing you do, to the point where you have both repeated to me an admonition I often directed at my mom: "Your opinion doesn't count because you love *everything* I do, say, am." That might bother you now, but get back to me when you're looking for unconditional love as an adult. You won't often find it, but you will always have that mother love—the certain knowledge deep down to the core of your being that you are truly cherished for exactly who you are.

Of course, Daddy and I have made sure you're surrounded by loving aunts, godmothers, neighbors, and our co-workers. If being fenced off from demoralizing forces was the sole guarantor of a happy, secure life, you two would have it all wrapped up. But it's not. All good parents and most schools do their best to provide secure surroundings, yet some kids flourish and others languish. Why? How do secure, loved kids turn into insecure, raving neurotics?

One answer might be that even great parents unwittingly pass on their anxieties to their kids. I had to really think about this when you were born. Getting my act together for myself was one thing, but before I went about the business of passing on these practical tips to you, I needed to make sure I wasn't passing on problems in the first place.

I'm not talking about those garden-variety insecurities. I mean wake-up-in-the-middle-of-the-night, heart-pounding, breath-shortening FREE-FLOATING ANXIETY. In a way I've only recently been coming to understand, my mother inadvertently passed on this distracting and destructive predilection. By shielding me from her fears and aloneness, she never let me know what powerful forces they could be or, more practically, how to deal with them. Ma's untimely death locked a certain fearsome loneliness inside me for all time.

Daddy picks at this lock all the time, and sometimes he can crack the code. But inside he'll find some empty space that only my mother could ever fill and explain.

I have waded through many mournful moments trying to purge this beast and have vowed that it would stop with me. Only my mother knew the deepest causes of her fear and loneliness. And though she never told me this in so many words, the root and depth of her demons likely led back to her own mother, who died at the painfully young age of forty-four after a slow, hard decline at home in my mother's care. Grandma had birthed a baby boy only six years before, at age thirty-eight, which wasn't typical of the times. I can only imagine the emotional and physical upheaval wrought by the collision of the unexpected blessing of a child and the equally unexpected sentence of death (for at that time, aggressive cancer meant, as it did for my mom, certain death).

My mother was catapulted overnight from the joys of a young marriage to the exhausting slog of caring for her mother's growing boy and wasting body. Surely Grandma Irene was scared; surely my mother had to have been terrified too. And overwhelmed by the life-and-death responsibilities that had landed on her overnight. And devastated at the prospect of being left alone to shoulder such burdens. Yet my mom never told me once that either she or her mother was ever scared. Even when Ma was on her own cancer death march, she never once admitted any fears. Even when I pointedly and directly asked her, "Are you scared?" "Of what?" she'd said. "Everything's gonna be fine."

I wish my mom had felt she was entitled to confess her panic over the prospect of death or even just the everyday anxieties of life. I wish we could have had soul-searching talks about both her and her mother; enduring so much, so young shaped them, and in turn, me. Maybe she thought such a confession would have been wimpy, whiny. More likely, she wanted to protect me from a pain she, like her mother, never faced but never escaped.

Because both my mother and grandmother led their lives denying the existence of their fear and loneliness most likely to themselves and certainly to their children, I grew up fundamentally ill-equipped to deal with or even name those same emotions when they inevitably turned up inside me. I could never understand why I'd be so haunted by insecurity and loneliness when I had all these accomplishments racked up on my résumé and the blessing of great friends and family.

As near as I can figure, and it's just a theory, I think I have this negative quality because of my perfect mom—or, more accurately, because I thought my mom was perfect. I was blind to her problems. Of course, she wasn't perfect—no one is—but I never, ever saw any flaws in her. To this day, I'm stunned and puzzled when moms tell me about their teenage daughter traumas. I never fought with Ma that I can remember beyond a brawl or two over boys (she had very high standards). In my eyes, Ma could do no wrong. To this day I can't fault her for trying to protect me.

Compounding my fantasy image of my mother was that reticence she had about discussing her feelings. Of course, her generation often kept their feelings to themselves, but she was really the queen of quiet when it came to her own trials. People brought their problems to her; she kept her problems to herself. Maybe my mother would have shared more of her personal struggles when I got old enough to understand them, but we never had that chance. I never learned how to discuss my "issues" comfortably or constructively, except with her. When I lost her, I lost my emotional compass, my source of validation.

The combination of my inability to see any imperfection in my mom and her protective instinct to shield me from any of her own scared feelings left me believing that it was possible to live a life untrammeled by insecurities, anxiety, fear, or loneliness. Small wonder I overreact to any normal sign of imperfection, in myself or others.

Although I've learned to deal with my own insecurity (sort of), I'm still haunted by the quest for some unobtainable perfection. You inherited my tendencies to be your own worst critic and to see those you love through rose-colored glasses, to overlook their flaws.

What I want you to know for your own personal growth is that I'm not perfect. I may be worrying here for nothing—what a surprise! I'm actually thrilled that you guys keep a running tally of my many flaws! In fact, everything that goes wrong around here is my fault! From the empty refrigerator to dorky clothes to dead hamsters to snarly hair. No wonder I have free-floating freak-outs! But hey, bring it on. Feel free to blame your mother! I wouldn't dream of denying you those typical mother-daughter "it's all your fault" fights! They're healthier than my never, ever blaming my mother for anything.

I don't mean blaming as in abdicating your own responsibility for developing emotional maturity. I mean taking note of whether you're unconsciously imitating what you were exposed to or reacting as your true self. This is why I'm always bugging you, "How do you feel? What are you thinking?" Hopefully we can put a dagger through the free-floating angst demon.

Let's get back to those "normal" freak-outs. Even if I *were* perfect—and of course, according to him, your father *is* perfect—*and* your home and school life were strife-free, *and* you succeeded at every endeavor you undertook, you would still have bouts of insecurity, because *everybody has bouts of insecurity*. So lighten up on yourself. It's easier to deal with your meltdowns if you know that everyone feels inadequate sometimes. Everyone. Just because people don't talk about it (see discussion on boys) doesn't mean they don't experience it. Whenever I'm in a new situation and am absolutely positive I'm going to make a fool of myself, I think of the late, great Lee Atwater, who told me that knowing that everybody is insecure sometimes was the secret to his success. Then I scan the room and imagine how these incredibly better-than-me people have insecurities too!

There's a reason everyone is insecure sometimes. New situations *are* always nerve-wracking, but there are ways to reduce near trauma to mere butterflies.

You can build your confidence with preparation. Organize your thoughts. Practice. Persevere. I often had massive anxiety attacks before I had to speak in public, until I realized that they only happened when my speech was pretty pathetic. When I pulled my thoughts and some facts together, I started having fun, even though I have no talent for public speaking, unlike your father, who was born to blab.

When you're in a new situation, take a moment to get the lay of the land; assess your surroundings. Look before you speak. Know your audience. Get comfortable, then behave appropriately to the environment. I don't mean go along to get along or just fit in by being like everyone else. I mean be your unique self in ways befitting your situation. Sometimes this will mean sitting on some great thoughts because it makes more sense to let someone else have the floor while you listen. Watch; there's always some jerk in every situation that has all the answers: He or she may be the smartest kid in the class, but it only counts if everyone knows it. Those kids grow up to be obnoxious, distracting rejects.

Figure out which environments you flourish in and which ones you can't get comfortable in, which energize and spark your best and which constipate your thought process.

Daddy and I are campaign people; we do our best work in unstructured, frenetic, pull-it-from-your-gut, shoot-from-the-hip, action/results-oriented, iconoclastic environments where trust, loyalty, and camaraderie are unquestioned. It's an honor and privilege to work in any White House, especially for leaders you really believe in, but toward the end of my White House tour of duty, I found myself remarking regularly to the vice president that I didn't have an "institutional constitution." I felt fundamentally ill equipped to function, or at least flourish, in the kind of highly structured setting necessary for a smoothly operating White House. I'm just not a "meeting" or a "memo" person. I'm a pace-around-the-room-shouting-ideas-and-acting-on-them person. That's no way to help a president serve the people, so I just didn't fit in. I remember sitting in the Roosevelt Room at the daily 7:30 AM senior staff meeting (no one should have to have her makeup and hair done by 7:30 AM every day) and feeling so out of place I would have out-of-body experiences. As the very organized Chief of Staff Andy Card politely canvassed the room one by one for updates from their offices, I would daydream nostalgically about everybody yelling at once, people throwing wadded up paper at co-workers who gave really dopey suggestions, a TV blaring in the background, hyper people coming in late and leaving early, and a *lot* of bad language. In short, a campaign meeting. When Andy called on me from my assigned antique wingback chair, I would snap out of it, but I either said nothing or something irreverent or irrelevant.

It's not that one working environment was better or worse, only that my work was better or worse depending on the environment. So the next time you feel uncomfortable or inappropriate or unproductive, before you dissolve into a Silly Putty of insecurity and self-blame, analyze the environment to see if the real problem is that you're the right person in the wrong place.

Thank goodness my actual White House job was more in the campaign mode. I had an officious title, but my function was offensive defense: to put out fires, troubleshoot, and pooper-scoop. Advanced pooper-scooping requires a certain level of frenzied and spontaneous thinking and a lot of shouting. It also gives you some leeway to say in-your-face things to the press that would be otherwise inappropriate for White House business. Generally, however, the White House is not a home for smart alecks and frenetics. I always tried to lower my voice and slow down to what looked something like the manner of an adult professional (especially with the president or vice president), but it was such an unnatural state that I lived every day in fear that I would pop off something that would embarrass them or me. Compare that work environment to that of a campaign or television program, where embarrassment, while nearly impossible, is in fact often the goal!

Let's suppose you *are* in the right place, but you're still a little wobbly. Faking it can work. My first mentor, Maxine Fernstrom, always said, "You become the way you behave." If you *act* like you're cool in a situation, you probably can be. If you act like you're in charge, you end up being in charge.

A cautionary note: Faking it doesn't work if you really are a fake. It's just a holding pattern until you get into position to deliver.

I always flashed back to Maxine whenever the vice president would unexpectedly throw me into a circumstance I considered beyond my capacity, like the time he had me address the cabinet at an energy task force meeting, or the time he got laryngitis and I had to give his speech (or my version of it) at a televised town hall meeting. My first feeling was voiced by retired Vice Admiral James Stockdale, Ross Perot's running mate, in his opening remarks during the 1992 vice-presidential debates: "Who am I? What am I doing here?" But my next thought was, Just act like you know what you're talking about! Again, this only works if you do know what to do when it comes time to actually do it.

You have to pay attention to your well-being to do well. Get a good night's sleep, eat decent food, enjoy some kind of physical activity beyond channel changing. You both are likely to lose it when you're tired, hungry, or bored. This isn't going to get better with age for you. Daddy and I both fritz if we don't stick to a healthy regimen.

And don't forget the x factor of your hormones, which can make you feel wildly off balance sometimes. It's up to you to get to know your body chemistry and how your emotions and performance respond to it.

Most important, when you're feeling freaked out, talk about it. Shine a light on those shadows, and know that the people you love will understand—and help you. Don't be afraid to show the chinks in your armor. Sharing your scary feelings with friends and family will deflate your fears and give you perspective. And don't be afraid to ask for help at school or work. People like to help, to pass on their knowledge; it makes them feel good. Don't worry about folks' passing judgment on your mistakes. Ma used to say, "Most people care more about their hangnails than your travails." She didn't say this to put others down but to reduce our adolescent self-consciousness.

Remember that not all insecure feelings are unhealthy. Feeling insecure can give you a "caution cushion"—a little look-before-you-leap space. Also, anxiety can be a great motivator. It gets your adrenaline pumping; it makes you more thorough. Best of all, if you were never insecure, you'd never have that great feeling that comes when you conquer your fears!

Finally, freaking out can be fun with your girlfriends or sister. Aunt Maria loves when I get hysterical so she can remind me, "You are *out of your mind!*" When Renie and I get especially worked up, we always end up sputtering something so utterly stupid that we bust out laughing.

Okay, perfect little lambs, you have much to give you confidence. You are bright and poised and kind. But you still have to deal with your DNA. You got one neurotic mother and one nutty daddy. But as Daddy points out, we have perfected our imperfections, if that's any consolation!

Flawfully yours,
Mom

My sister, Irene "Renie" O'Brien,
and myself, Hurricane Isabel,
September 2003.

AFTER THE FLOOD

Dear Aqua-Girls,

Usually too hyper for TV, Daddy was glued to, of all things, the *Weather Channel*. He's always been a weird weather-watching junkie, but now he was a man on a mission. Hurricane Isabel was out at sea circling herky-jerky over those abstract satellite presentations, and the earnest forecasters were predicting Armageddon. When Daddy forces me to watch the weather with him, all I see are moving colors on a map. He sees wind, rain, snow, high pressure, low pressure, cloud formations, gathering threats, moving fronts. Just another example of how differently we see one world!

Whenever Daddy is superconcerned, he gets extremely focused, which produces a calmness startling in its contrast to his usual manner. Daddy's intense focus on Hurricane Isabel was clearly motivated by more than his usual Weather Channel obsession. I told him, "James, snap out of it," one of my oft-used mantras. He said, "This could be, in fact, probably *will* be a disaster for us." I'm used to Daddy predicting weather calamities for his beloved Louisiana, but this time he meant us, as in *us*. In Virginia. In a suburb of the nation's capital—a place that barely has seasons, let alone Weather Channel superstars! I try not to be dismissive of Daddy's many idiosyncrasies and icono-clastic interests (sure, it's slightly odd to watch your hus-band lip-sync every line from *The Andy Griffith Show*), and though he qualifies as a hurricane expert, in this case his disaster prediction seemed totally far-fetched. Besides, I didn't need one more thing to worry about. My brother was in the hospital, I'd started work on a new TV show, school had begun, my manuscript was late, and White House wartime issues were increasingly negative. I was in no mood and had no room in my brain to indulge one of Daddy's oddball concerns.

So all week long, as Isabel raged up the eastern seaboard, Daddy grew more agitated and I more apathetic. He called our buddy Dave, who knows how to do every-thing, and asked him to nail plywood over our doors and windows. I called Dave and told him over my dead body would we ply my brand-new French doors!

Then Daddy told Dave to sandbag our front and back entrances. I threw a hissy fit over the silliness of his prepa-rations for what I was sure would end up being nothing but a little rain and wind. I consoled myself that at least the kids could play in the sand afterward. Despite my week-long eye rolling over Daddy's hurricane hypochondria, I did get into the spirit the evening before Isabel was supposed to hit us and pulled together a Hurricane Happy Hour for our best pals and neighbors, Maria and Ann. To my utter amazement (and horror), my gal pals indulged Daddy's Big Wind fantasies. Only big wine could make them shut up about the stupid weather.

That happy (several) hour(s) produced a wake-up headache at 2:19 AM. Downing a couple of Advils at the bedroom window, I took great pleasure in noting that not a leaf was stirring, not a drop of rain was falling. I even woke Daddy up to make fun of him. He didn't consider that appropriate wifely affection, so I thought it was payback when he woke *me* up forty minutes later to say that Aunt Maria next door had called to say that the weather might be kicking up and maybe we should check our ground floor. I smashed a pillow over my head(ache), but since I love Maria, I told Daddy to go look downstairs so he could call her back and reassure her all was fine.

Wearing his special SpongeBob SquarePants boxers from Tar-jhay, Daddy descended two floors to the ground floor to check on his beloved "womb room," his sanity haven, his sanctum sanctorum. The man's room, in a house of all girls—including pets! Almost the entire floor had been meticulously outfitted just for him: custom-made sofa, granite bar, giant plasma TV, hand-tooled walnut wainscot and floor-to-ceiling cabinetry, the cushiest carpet you ever rolled around on, a hand-carved African bench, every TV gizmo ever invented, all his methodically chosen reference books, signed sports memorabilia, an expansive stash of Maker's Mark minibottles, a plush Italian leather easy chair, many pieces of Italian ceramic and English crystal, and some original Russian paintings I got in only because they weren't "girly-girl."

Daddy shouted up, "Maybe you should come down here." Chalking it up to more hurricane hysteria, I huffily pounded down the stairs in my usual enticing nighttime attire of men's bottoms and a workout shirt.

Looking down from the top of the stairs, I saw nothing but our perfectly clean black and white marble floor. So the trip wouldn't be a total waste of time and because I was pissed off, I figured I'd puff on downstairs to the first floor and get on Daddy (okay, now I owe you twenty-five cents for a potty word).

But when I saw Daddy's expression, I went from pissed to perplexed. He was watching brown, smelly water slowly oozing from under the first floor door leading to the garage. We had no idea where this ooze was coming from, but we trudged back upstairs to get some bath towels to soak up the mess. We'd only gotten up one flight to the next floor when we found (and how they got there, I still do not know) thigh-high-rubber-booted fire marshals swarming through our front door, pushing past Daddy, still bedecked in his boxers, ordering us "out of the flood floor!" politely, but in no uncertain terms. I was still slightly woozy from the hurricane party and couldn't figure out what was going on.

"Ma'am, we're here to help you." One of the fire marshals was a woman. I was pleased and impressed, but my "I-am-woman-I-am-strong" moment was cut short when that female firmly moved me aside to get down to the first floor. Shaking off my stupor, I followed hot on her heels down the same staircase I'd just ascended. At the foot of the stairs, we discovered that the black and white marble foyer had in the space of a few minutes become a reservoir of brown, mucky, smelly water, and the trickle of ooze under the door had become a waterfall gushing around *all sides* of the door. The muck in the foyer was at least a foot deep and rising fast. At this moment, it occurred to me in a jolt of materialistic panic that this floor housed more than Daddy's deliverance room. My spare closet was down here. All my coats (fur, cashmere, leather, dress-up, and wraps) and all my formals (silk, lace, and velvet gowns) and all my boots (designer, hikers, and heels). I pushed past the female firefighter to the coveted closet. Mucking through in my bare feet, with the specific mission of retrieving my sable-lapelled ankle-length sheared mink, I grabbed an armload of coats. A rubber-booted male marshal joined his partner; both ordered me, loudly, out of the water, which was already up to my knees. "Get out. You're gonna get electrocuted. Get out of the water, *now!*" I didn't actually consciously choose between being electrocuted and losing my coats, but after carefully hanging the mink in a safe, dry place, some primal force propelled me back to the closet for another load.

This time the marshals were seriously mad. "We can arrest you or evacuate you. This is for your own good." As the foul-smelling muck plastered my soaking pajama bottoms into the cellulite of my upper legs—my God, how had it risen so quickly?—I began to appreciate why the marshals were wearing *thigh*-high boots. I must have seemed equal parts demonic and pathetic. They took pity on my wretched state.

"We'll help you." They started pulling art off the walls and retrieving Italian ceramics floating through the muck. I screamed, "My coats, my coats!" They hauled out another load from the closet, which was no small feat since they had to heft the heavy, waterlogged load overhead while wading through the thigh-high sludge and dodging various pieces of floating furniture. Even as I was greedily grabbing their load, I screamed again (which even at the time I registered as a sign of mental illness), "Go back down and get the reversible red leather!"

Only as I was carefully placing the reversible red leather with the other heroically (if insanely) retrieved items did it occur to me that there was no reason, other than my total derangement, for me to be screaming at those good people. I truly appreciate their preventing my electrocution, and I'd like to take this opportunity to especially thank the fire marshals of Alexandria, Virginia, for not slapping me at that moment.

I ran up to the second-floor porch to see what had caused this mess. Outside the wind was roaring, debris was flying through the air, and a waterfall was rushing onto our street. At the high end of the block, I could see Maria and our friend Sarah racing against the shrieking wind to move all our cars before they floated away with the others already bobbing around the bottom of the block. They'd scarcely returned from around the corner before the entire block was completely underwater.

Your Aunt Maria is none too tall, and I was afraid she might get swept away in the torrents. I found myself screaming her name over and over, "Maria, Maria!"

"I'm over here. Stop screaming!" she screamed from her second-floor porch.

My newly tapestried ottoman floated by on a torrent of brown muck. I screamed, "Maria, my furniture is in your first floor!"

She screamed, "You want your [expletive deleted] furniture? There's your [expletive deleted] furniture!" while flailing her arms at my sofa bed bobbing past her window.

I was about to assess her fifty cents for two potty words (plus a penalty fifty cents for extra-bad words) when I saw all of her beloved artwork floating along with my sofa.

Maria and I, best friends for over two decades, burst out laughing and crying then. Daddy calmly started serving everyone freshly brewed French-pressed coffee. Yankees and southerners respond differently under stress.

The voyage on the Townhouse Titanic had taken less than an hour, so it was only a little after 4 AM when I woke you guys before all the noise did. Desperate to prepare you for the devastation, I hugged and kissed you as we walked downstairs. At the sight of both your house and street under water, you both said the same thing at the same time, with the same engaged expression: "*Cooooool!*"

When you're looking to regain your perspective, it doesn't get any better than that.

Let's stop here to distill the life lessons of the story so far:

1. Take "Weather Channel watching" off the list of things about which to make fun of Daddy.
2. Parties are not the best preparation for hurricanes.
3. Never go to a flood in bad pajamas.
4. Coffee trumps crying.
5. Thigh-high rubber boots are more than a fashion statement.

6. For the best perspective on the loss of material stuff, go to a five- and an eight-year-old.

THE FLOOD—DAY 2

Actually, it was still Day 1. Everything that seemed so surreal during the night became all too real by day. Isabel had struck the Potomac River at high tide, producing a storm surge of over nine feet that burst through the Jones Point Seawall. Our block had become a tributary of the Potomac. The outsized tide was awash with everyone's earthly possessions, giant tree limbs felled by the wind, and a goodly number of sports cars. The street lake had receded with the tide, turning our townhouse development's underground garage into our own special pool. As we neighbors looked on, dumbstruck and numb, gawkers slogged through the debris, cameras in hand.

Oddly, and in an out-of-body way, I was supremely polite and informative to the hordes chronicling our devastation. You two were superb entertainers, donning the official hats and rubber boots (those fabulous fashion statements!) of the firefighters. The "audience" snapped photos of you posing with the fire chief in front of a fallen street sign.

Gaggles of neighbors gathered streetside to exchange practical information, no one able to fathom the depth of their losses yet. We couldn't even get into our garages to assess the damage since the weight of the deep water made it impossible to open the doors.

Only after the garage reservoir had been drained several feet were we able to push through to our garages, where another surreal surprise awaited us. As we peered into the darkness, we saw giant ponds stocked with all our stuff floating like dead fish, bloated in unnatural positions. The power outage had caused every individual electric garage door to pop open, so random items from every garage converged in this impromptu conversation pit. Dimly I saw all our patio cushions bobbing among mattresses, golf clubs, books, brooms, toys, furniture, and other tokens from dozens of lifetimes. Still in denial at the destruction, I insanely consoled myself with the fact that the cushions were waterproof, willfully ignoring all the rest of the floating damage.

Aunt Renie and her son Kevin somehow navigated the closed parkway between our homes to help me get my bearings. Though we still were getting electrocution warnings, Renie and I ventured into the nearly pitch-dark garage cesspool to see what we might salvage. As Renie, standing knee-deep in dirty muck, tipped the filthy water out of a box, out came a huge, wriggling monster. I couldn't tell whether it was a snake, eel, or other horror, but as it flopped against my bare leg, the one thing I knew for sure was that it was positively, decidedly *alive*. It slithered away fast, which in no way mitigated my terror.

Screaming, thrashing, splashing my sister, I skedaddled out of that garage lagoon and retired to Maria's porch with a bottle of champagne and a Domino's pizza. (Domino's is right up there, reliabilitywise, with the United States Postal Service.)

THE FLOOD — DAY 2 FOR REAL

I woke with a heavy heart and spinning head to a miraculously brilliant blue, sunny day. I can't start the day without coffee. Strong coffee. When I brew it, I fill the French press pot almost halfway with fresh grounds. This morning, though, we'd been told our water was too contaminated to drink, so I sent Daddy down to Starbucks for a four-shot Venti skim latte, which would have saved the day, except that Starbucks had been flooded out of existence!

I actually started sucking on some coffee beans but then decided to be strong. I spotted a gallon of bleach with a sunflower tucked into its handle. Maria had left it for me—one of her typical gestures of optimism as we faced the unfathomable cleanup. We were told we had to bleach the entire first floor and everything in it to contain the contamination.

Filling my pockets with coffee beans, I decided to head over to Little Miss Sunshine Maria's townhouse next door, cutting through the underground passageway to avoid the hordes of filming gawkers who still lined our street. This was a mistake.

The garages were now lit; the water level was down to a foot or so. Below and above that foot, upside down and every which way, was every single item from our downstairs, including Daddy's cherished room, my exercise room, and your play room. Books, bikes, pots, pans, lamps, rugs, scooters, brooms, buckets, tables, vases, videos, tools. Bags of exploded kitty litter and puffed-up Kibbles 'n Bits. Clothes, clothes, and more clothes—yours, Daddy's, mine, Goodwill's. Your previously plush ABC carpet, the Cuisinart, cookie cutters, Cutty Sark. Decorations from Christmas, Thanksgiving, Halloween; baking dishes, birthday bows, and Easter baskets. Our Italian armoire, TVs, stereos, brand-new bedroom furniture, antique cabinets, a treadmill and elliptical trainer, our wine collection, sixteen pieces of top-of-the-line luggage. The list went on, but I was too shell-shocked to keep cataloguing it at the time. Anything still underwater was disintegrating; everything floating above it was coated with a stinky, poo-colored river slime.

When I saw all your favorite toys, including the ones I'd saved from your infancy on, I started to cry. I jumped into the mess to save some little baby-doll blankets Aunt Dorothy made, but I didn't know if they were salvageable. There was more chest heaving when I saw your cherished baby photos, destroyed. But what really pushed me over the edge were your flower-girl dresses—whispering white satin, silk, and linen confections you'd worn to weddings for Caroline, Dalit, John Orzag, Tom and Beth, and Merrill—all streaked and soaked in brown puke. I just started bawling.

This was our third move. We'd finally found our perfect family home. I'd restructured and redecorated our brand-new house inside out. The construction crews had literally just finished the day before the flood. The last down-filled pillow with my carefully chosen fabric had been plopped into place.

For months I'd been practically living with super-designers Bud and Ed, combing through interior design magazines, shopping with the concentration of a brain surgeon for the perfect rugs, furniture, lamps, wallpaper. Even the ceilings got special attention. Linda the artist had painted my favorite Marc Chagall mermaid on the kitchen ceiling à la Michelangelo.

This—our final home—was my masterpiece! My pièce de résistance! My feng shui grand finale!

Daddy had a slightly different view of my extreme home makeover. To him, it was an extraordinary money pit. We'd developed a family ritual. Daddy never stopped complaining about how much I spent on the house. He would walk around and pick up vases and push around chairs, chanting "How much did *this* cost?" He treated tchotchkes that I'd scoured the globe for like the Ebola virus. But then he would escort anyone and everyone who entered *his* home (including virtual strangers) throughout the house showing off the art, rugs, fixtures, woodwork, etc. He was very proud of his house.

This is a man thing. The woman thing is making a home. My job was to envelop us with inviting art; embracing, inspiring colors; comforting rugs; interesting fabrics and textures—creating the place that you would always want to come home to and that, more important, would be there for you far into your futures.

I'd always longed to create a space that perfectly reflected my idea of home. Sometimes to lull myself to sleep, I would visualize each room of Gram's house: the colors, the furniture, the sunlight through the back windows, the pantry. I remember when she had a real ice box! I do the same mental tour of my mother's house. I remember her on her hands and knees stripping the varnish off the woodwork; scrubbing the bathroom fixtures with a toothbrush; ironing in the front room, spritzing a Coke bottle of water over each wrinkled piece. Before dryers, she would wring our wash through the kind of hand crank you only see in antique shops. Then she'd hang the laundry on a clothesline in the back yard. In Ma's house, the beds were never unmade, the dishes always done. Once she redecorated the living room and left plastic covers on the couch. She always shooed us out of this room—"I want to keep it nice for the preacher to visit"—though I don't remember any such a visit. Once she stripped all the old front room tables and painted them a saucy red.

In an effort to teach us both homemaking and independence, Ma let my sister and me redo our rooms. Renie painted hers yellow and placed black footprints up the walls and across the ceiling. I meticulously mapped out an American flag in a circle and painstakingly painted it in. This was not a positive harbinger of my future design capabilities, but I loved the process of converting a space to *my* place.

When Daddy and I found our dream house, I felt I finally had a chance to make our home into the place you two would visit in your dreams as you lulled yourselves to sleep. I felt we'd finally achieved our perfect nest, and then Hurricane Isabel swept it all away.

Or so I thought.

As it turns out, Isabel was a special gift. We all know that the stuff in a house isn't what makes it a home. After my initial mourning period, I was gratified to discover how little any of it meant to any of us. After the dust settled, what you two concentrated on was helping Aunt Maria and me rebuild—keeping us company while we cleaned up; sweeping, dusting, painting with us; laughing at our endless flood stories. You went out of your way to compliment our progress, to get excited with us as the walls went back up, even though, I know, this was boring for you. You were empathetic and sensitive and gracious beyond your years. You helped us remember that we'd never lost anything that really mattered.

The experience of seeing us lose our shared space helped you developed a new respect for your own. You now meander around your rooms, rearranging the furniture, hanging up new pictures. You no longer make fun of me when I stand and stare at a room in a trance, waiting for the feng shui vibe to hit me. You now see what I used to see—our home.

And now I see our home in your little hearts.

That is homemaking.

XOXO,
Mom

P.S. Now that you like to go home shopping with me, you must take my sacred "inferior desecrators" pledge: never tell Daddy how much anything costs.

SOUL SISTERS

Dear Girlfriends,

By geographic accident, I grew up without girlfriends. Our parentally mandated play radius—a mere two blocks—was populated with many boys of all ages and no girls my age, so all my buds were boys. We remained best friends until our emerging gender differences became too evident to ignore. That is to say, I got, among other things, boobs (an enduring gender difference that men never ignore). I didn't even notice those boobs until one day while climbing a tree with the guys, I got kicked in one. I climbed down and never went back up.

As our bodies developed with the onslaught of puberty, the bonds with my boy buds unraveled. With no warning, no discussion, and no comprehension, friendships forged as toddlers disintegrated. Still, those formative years and

*My mother, Eileen Emerson Matalin (front row, second from right),
with her girlfriends, circa 1947.*

friendships gave me an insight and appreciation of boys I don't think I could ever have gotten otherwise.

What I missed in girlfriendhood, I made up in adventures. The boys and I were more rowdy than the few girls in the neighborhood, more competitive about everything, more physical, more curious about weird things (like how to detach the fire from the firefly), less afraid of dangerous things (like railroad tracks). We played football in the front street, basketball in the back yard. We rode cardboard boxes down big hills and dug through broken beer bottles, discarded by litterbugs in the neighborhood empty lot, to make cool forts.

I don't remember ever combing my hair, caring about clothes, yakking on the phone, trading shoes, or "liking" boys—all hallmarks of your everyday lives. My mom and my sister were my best and only girlfriends, and they were the best, period.

Now, through you, I can see what I missed out on. Even though they do have the raw material for friendships postpuberty, boys can rarely be the kind of soul-mate buddies that girls can be, because the essence of what makes a man a man and a woman a woman can only be truly understood by people of the same gender. This isn't to say we can't grasp the basics of our other-gendered fellow humans; it's just that we're different from stem to stern, and what defines us is in many ways ultimately "ungettable" by the other sex.

Over time, much time, I've learned to understand what makes your dad tick, and he has done the same for me, and we love each other in spite of it! But I do not, cannot, and desire not to know what it means to be a man. Close as we are, we simply cannot scratch each other's every itch. At certain times Daddy just says, "You need to call your sister" or "You need to go see Maria." And he finds it simply unfathomable that I can spend two or three hours on the phone with Jill or Grace talking about nothing and everything.

Just as I cannot fathom how recounting twenty-year-old World Series play-by-plays could interest anyone, ever. Yet Daddy and Jon Macks can revel in these memories interminably. And what's with spending hours looking at new cars you're never going to buy? And when do men ever give up sharing the "joys" of girlie magazines? And, really, how many times can you watch *The Godfather*, in the same day?

Well, however different Daddy and I are, we both know this: we love our best friends. As girls, you may have friends who are boys, but you will bond differently and more deeply with your girlfriends.

You'll always need to analyze why you love your husband, because if you have a normal marriage, you'll find yourself asking (often) why you love him, how you could possibly love him, what you see in him. You'll have to memorize your answers to deploy during times of irresolvable conflict.

You'll never need to analyze why you love your children, because you will never not love them without reservation. (You may momentarily not like them much, but you'll still love them.) Even in the worst head-butting times with your kids, you'll never consider the possibility that you won't be able to bridge your differences or repair the damage to your relationship, no matter how major your disputes.

You'll never be able to analyze why you love your best girlfriends. Sure, you'll be able to list their attributes—Maria's thoughtfulness, Jill's loyalty, Gracie's strength—but those won't explain why you love them. You'll love them because you just do. It just is what it is. You can't parse the soul of a soul sister. You will have many pals (even casual girlfriends are joys) but precious few soul sisters. Take care of and treasure these relationships.

My mom had a bunch of girlfriends from grade school she kept all her life. Even with Ma gone, those women still hang together, and they love you two as they did my brother, sister, and me, as they did their own kids. They have shared each other's lives. Judging from the amount of time they spent on the phone, they practically *lived* each other's lives. My mom never gabbed on the phone when my dad was home, but the second he was out the door in the morning, she started in with her coffee, cigarettes, and a round of girlfriend calls. I never saw my mom laugh in any other situation as freely as she did with her gal pals.

Without your asking, your girlfriends will always be there, supporting you, sharing with you, protecting you, accepting you, creating adventures with you, pursuing new interests. They'll embrace you when you've been done wrong and make you face it when you do wrong.

There are many girls-only topics on which guys check out. You can already see how clueless they are about the major crushes you have on them. The older you get, the more clueless they get on your critical issues. You'll always want a few boy friends—as opposed to boyfriends— around as sounding boards or reality checks, but it's the girlfriends who will turn any event, good or bad, into a get-down-girl, 100 percent estrogen, chocolate-chip pig-out or coffee klatch or winefest.

Boys don't have the requisite metabolism for discussing the same topic for hours, like the way you and your girl-friends can already devote all night to what teachers you got and who's in your classes and who picked whom to sit by in the cafeteria. As you grow with your girlfriends, you'll find yourselves devoting the same level of attention to the details of everything from finding a new hairdresser to dealing with some jerk at work stealing one of your ideas and passing it off as his own.

Even if they learn how to pretend to be interested in

your issues, boys will never "get" them, the life-and-death issues like zits or bad hair or PMS. They think feng shui is Chinese takeout. They expend no psychic energy on back-stabbers or blabbermouths at work; they just move on.

Not that they don't have their own form of communicating or sharing emotion. Whenever Daddy and I have a doozy of a battle, he calls Tim and talks about sports for about ten minutes. I call Jill, and a couple of hours later we've covered every nuance of every argument each of us has had for the last five years.

For happy events, even milestones, boys simply announce whatever it is and move on. Take getting married: how could you just announce you're getting married without covering—in great detail—the actual proposal, the ring, dress, wedding menu, invitation list, flowers, and your specific plans for the rest of your married life?

Babies? Men do mention "boy" or "girl," but where's the blow-by-blow of labor? The minute-to-minute description of baby's growth? The worrying about college the day baby is born?

And how come they never tear up over anything? While we do over almost everything?

You could spend your entire postpubescent life trying to figure why your girlfriends "get it" and why boys are so seemingly dense. I'm gonna save you a lot of brain drain and exasperation: don't bother. It doesn't matter. You will connect with the boys you fall for and connect deeply with your life mate, but your bond with your soul sisters is like no other.

You're already learning about the importance of girl-friends by watching me with my friends, by just being there with us. Already you two join in our all-girl gabfests. You have that natural rhythm women fall into when we're getting our hair or nails done, when total stranger girls engage in intense conversation. Best of all, you already cherish your special girl buddies. Both of you are friendly and outgoing to all but have chosen your best buds with great care. You're already learning the most important lesson: best buddies are sacred.

I'd be remiss, though, if I didn't tell you that girls can also be your worst nightmare. Some girls are born bitches. They're just mean. They use and torment people for the hell of it. It's shocking to see it happening at your young ages, but I guess that proves they're born hardwired to be hags. I cannot explain them. I've been telling you they're just sad kids—and they will end up sad—but I really don't know. It's not worth trying to figure out. Just stay away. Even when they're "popular" girls. When these girls prey on you (and they will because you're so trusting), remember what my Ma always said, "What goes around, comes around."

To be honest with you, I never found Ma's advice there very helpful. I was always more of an "eye for an eye" kind of gal. But she was right, because plotting payback wastes too much energy and keeps you too focused on the negative.

Relationships can become especially difficult when you hit middle school, which—no coincidence here—happens to coincide with puberty, which can turn the slightest slights into emotional upheavals. High school is a hormone Hiroshima. Both boys and girls are continually off balance, but strangely, boys are better behaved when it comes to friendships. (They're out of their minds over girls, but that's another topic.)

Girls negotiate more shifting alliances than Bismarck. Best friends forever change on a dime; cliques merge and explode. Girls in pursuit of popularity routinely commit acts from petty to ghastly. From what I read, it's worse today because you are exposed to so much more, so much earlier. Parents are more permissive. I'm having a hard time telling high school girls from show girls. Peer pressure and the horror of anything other than uncompromising conformity to "cool" drives even sensible girls over the edge. You can be exiled from your clique, dumped by your best friend, turned into a total cootie overnight for the sin of pursuing a unique interest or having an independent thought.

A couple of things to remember: (1) This adolescent girl insanity is temporary; and (2) it's not about you, it's about an age. You shouldn't do anything or befriend anyone just to be popular. If it doesn't feel right or natural, it isn't and won't work. In the end, truly popular kids are the ones truest to themselves. They aren't sorting through friends and shifting opinions to be popular; they're popular because they are consistent, loyal, trustworthy.

If you're true to yourself, you'll attract the same kind of friends, and they will be true friends. You'll still have the occasional fracas with them (I still do with my buds), but you'll work through your conflicts and have an even stronger bond.

Even when you choose and treat your friends with care, you may still experience an irreparable falling-out with a girlfriend—a truly horrible experience, especially if she broke a trust. Somehow betrayal by a girlfriend is far worse than by a boyfriend.

When you're older, girls sometimes betray each other over a boyfriend. (I remember almost nothing about high school except how my best friend stole my first upperclassman boyfriend. That wench I can recall in Technicolor.) Every situation is unique, but my general advice is *never* trade a girlfriend for a boy, and *never* keep a best friend who steals your boyfriend. While we're on that topic, a boy who cheats on his girlfriend with her girlfriend is probably not a guy you want to keep around either.

It's okay to hand off a boyfriend. Daddy's nephews have an inviolate rule that none of them can ever go out with any of the others' previous girlfriends. Must be a boy thing. It's a little tricky, but if you're really over the boy, trading beaus is great fun.

You'll probably see movies and read stories about girlfriends betraying each other at work. That's never actually happened to me. In fact, my girlfriends and I have gone out on limbs for each other. If a girlfriend ever stabs you in the back at work, she wasn't your girlfriend. My work experience has been that women actually brag about the work of other women—unsolicited. If a girlfriend sees something amiss in your work, she'll figure out a way to diplomatically help you.

My White House gal pal and co-worker Karen Hughes and I had a virtual tag team between our West Wing offices—fleshing out each other's ideas, undoing dumb ones, or blowing off steam before we bit off someone's head. Either she would storm into my office and slam the door or I into hers and let loose. We'd race in with a new idea that *just had to be dealt with right then,* paying no attention to or interrupting whatever was going on. We conspired to push ideas we liked and head off ones we didn't.

I'm not saying you'll never have close male colleagues, but you won't punctuate your work with running commentary on kids, hair, home, pets, jewelry, shopping bargains, and husbands. My conversations with Karen would ricochet from the women of Afghanistan to finding a third workout partner. Maria and I have not had one single conversation about the 2004 elections without sidetracking to wallpaper, paint color, or whatever's the latest in our ongoing simultaneous redecorating.

There was a day—and not that very long ago—when "real women" proved their feminist bona fides by discussing only big ideas with other females. Everyday topics were oh so provincial and un-pro-gres-sive. I remember marching for the first Earth Day pretending I hadn't fussed with my hair all morning. I was dying to ask but didn't, God forbid, where did a fellow marcher get that fabulous faux lamb coat?

Let me tell you something, girls: just *living* is a big idea. Getting through each day with grace is a big idea.

The best way to make a big life is with the little chatter, small kindnesses, instinctive support, and unerring understanding of girlfriends.

So here's to gggrrrrrlll power,
Mom

LOYALTY

Dear Girls,

If there's one virtue that's first among equals, it's loyalty. Loyal relationships, whether they're one on one or with legions of people, always add up to a whole greater than the sum of its parts. Loyalty not only enhances human relationships, it can catapult groups of normal people to greatness in every endeavor from sports teams to empires.

If you think I'm exaggerating, analyze any good relationship; read the history of great nations. Heck, just study any winning team.

Since you follow so much news, much of which suggests that loyalty is passé, I want to make sure you understood that those high-profile examples of betrayal (the church, the heads of corporations and mutual funds run amok) are, I pray, aberrations. If not, those institutions are doomed. I want you to grasp the significance and necessity of loyalty in every day of our lives.

Fortunately, you are hardwired for loyalty. Your parents, as did their parents and grandparents, place a high premium on loyalty. My mom and dad were unswervingly loyal to their fellow workers, their employers, their friends, their neighbors. They were even devoted to their inanimate workplaces, the steel mill and beauty school.

People *are* less committed today, probably because we live in a far more mobile society. We don't put down roots like my parents' generation. We chase after job opportunities to advance our careers or provide for our families. But what we're gaining in employment opportunity, we're losing in workplace loyalty. Without some serious, conscious effort, we could also lose cohesive communities and even families.

Since you'll spend a big chunk of your life in workplace environs, let's cover professional loyalty first.

I was really lucky to have had some extraordinary role models and experiences that were steeped in loyalty. Political campaigns provide a fertile environment for this quality. There may be a campaign that succeeds without a loyal team, but I've never seen one. My old boss was the late, great Lee Atwater, campaign manager extraordinaire. For him, success depended not just on his own strategic genius but on legions of loyal supporters. His key management technique was to make his people loyal. He always said he'd rather hire a loyal rank amateur and train him or her than an expert with fidelity to no one.

The bonds of loyalty are a critical component of developing and maintaining motivation, which in turn are the key to any successful operation, especially competitive ones. Soldiers always cite loyalty to their buddies as *the* motivating force they needed to overcome extraordinary dangers or to forge cohesion for victories. Atwater studied every leader and military figure, especially conquering ones, throughout history. Everyone thought he was looking for a new competitive strategy. He would quote Sun Tzu or Attila the Hun or Michael Shaara to psyche out his opponents and make them think he was a superior student of strategy. But the real value he took from his studies was the knowledge of how to build and maintain a highly motivated team. At this he was the undisputed master. To this day political junkies regularly regale me with their unfaded memories of Atwater antics.

Atwater developed loyalty on a massive scale by working at an individual level. In the main, he begat loyalty by giving it. Atwater took care of his people. He got them jobs, promotions, raises. He gave them attention and credit (for even the tiniest achievements). He brought them to meetings and singled them out to bigwigs. He bragged about them to reporters and instigated more than a few personal profiles. He made sure President George Bush knew all his key people and that everyone had a signed photo. He watched your back and was your front-line defense for any attack.

No act of stupidity could dislodge Atwater's loyalty, but a single act of disloyalty meant certain disavowal. Atwater didn't waste time on revenge for disloyalty, since being on Lee's bad list was payback enough, but he did have a favorite ploy for losers who feigned loyalty. He made fools of them, less for retaliation than for his personal amusement. Like Daddy, Lee was amazed and amused by fools. Maybe it's a southern thing.

The greatest reward of Atwater's insistence on loyalty was the 1988 victory of the vice president, George Bush. Winning campaigns always look easy after the fact, but that one teetered on the edge. Yes, Lee pulled some grand strategic moves, but from my vantage point, the reason we carried the day was that he created a team of outstanding loyalty—a dedicated roster of folks who would walk through walls for him. Loyalty to Lee and the team kept us tough and tenacious.

We all worked every day with Lee, but what sustained our larger sense of purpose was loyalty to our candidate. Everyone loved George Herbert Walker Bush. A lot of his campaign people had been with him for decades, through the good and bad and ugly. Poppy's people are still, and will always be, Poppy's people. Our loyalty then and continued fidelity was not based on sycophantism or ideological fanaticism. In fact, he attracted neither suck-ups nor fanatics. What he did attract, and what he embodied, was deep, dense loyalty.

A good time to take the measure of a loyal relationship is when things aren't going as planned—more precisely, when stuff is hitting the fan. It's easy to throw your lot in with a winner; it's harder to be loyal in a losing situation. The true test of loyalty is allegiance when all appears lost. In 1992 we were veritably racing downhill from the minute we opened our campaign headquarters. We pounded into one catastrophe after another—most not of our making and beyond our control. Campaign people are superstitious. Our lead adviser, Charlie Black, chalked our daily disasters up to our being "snakebit"; whatever the reason, the election gods had turned against us.

The worse it got, the dumber I got. Once I pulled a stupid stunt by drawing attention to our opponent's "bimbo eruptions," which threw our campaign into disarray and had their campaign calling for my head. President Bush not only wouldn't fire me, he sent the signal to our own guys to lighten up on me. I was crying, sobbing, offering to resign, and he just told me to soften up a bit!

At the same time that I was working myself into a (stupid) frenzy, I was shocked at how many rats were jumping ship, trashing the campaign, and worse, the candidate, in the media—anonymously, of course. Cowardly rats. It's one thing to have internal come-to-Jesus meetings; it's treason to tattle to the press.

Campaign analysis tip: Whenever you see or hear any media quoting "campaign sources" attacking others on their own campaign, defeat is knocking on the door. You can apply this to most any project where humans team up—from sports to TV shows to businesses to wars. When loyalty to the cause or leader lapses, the vacuum left by the absence of a cohesive force of loyalists is filled by self-interested individuals. These selfish black holes are a pretty powerful source too, to which the weak and scared gravitate. Before you know it, the whole production implodes. Let's call it the Reverse Loyalty Effect.

We were swimming against the tide to start with in 1992, but what finally took us under was the every-man-for-himself syndrome.

How could the same candidate/cause be so successful in one election and completely disastrous in the next? There were many negative external factors, but to me it appeared that a key destructive force was internal. What happened between the 1988 and 1992 campaigns was the dissolution of loyalty, or at least loyalty to a cause larger than oneself. There was plenty of personal fidelity to the president in 1992, but there were more folks working in the 1992 campaign who were using it as a career jumping stone than who cared about President Bush, and it showed.

The core Bushies never wavered. By any objective standard, we were losing, but our eleventh-hour loyalty call gave us hope, confidence, resolve. And President Bush never lost his loyalty to his team. I was always screaming about the rats; he was preternaturally gracious to everyone. We leftover loyalists on *Air Force One* banded together like those lost Japanese soldiers who stayed on an island long after World War II ended, unaware that the conflict was over, determined to keep their island secure. We played cards, sang songs, snapped the heads off any media that put out bad stories—which was all media. We became a solid, protective phalanx spitting nails at the naysayers. We were going to win.

Every day I would bring the worst polls to President Bush's office cabin and ferret through them for any positive movement, however minute. I swore to him we were winning. I promised we would win. At 5 PM on Election Day, when all the exit polls had us tanked, I went on *Larry King Live* and trilled, "We're winning! We're winning!"

And then we lost.

On the day after the election, en route from our concession "party" in Houston to the mourning White House, President Bush walked through *Air Force One* thanking each and every one of us. Telling us what a great job we'd done. Consoling *us*.

When he saw me, he laughed. "We're winning, we're winning!" Years afterward, every time we see each other, he laughs and says, "We're winning, we're winning!" You know what? I look back and know I *did* win, because that campaign showed me—every day—how to be loyal.

Of your dad's many attributes, high on my list is his limitless capacity for loyalty. If Daddy is on your side, as one of my favorite loyal buddies, Torie Clarke, used to say, "he'd crawl over broken glass on a four-lane highway at rush hour."

You were too young to remember Daddy's greatest, most outrageous act of loyalty. Emma was a newborn, so I was home all day watching cable TV. In response to my screaming at Daddy on TV as he was defending Bill Clinton, Matty would just say, "You shouldn't lie under the oak," her version of the principle embodied in the story of Washington's chopping down the cherry tree.

Maybe you'll learn about it in school. It was a bad time for the country, for politics, and for us. I cried a lot. Some of the time I was crying because I was so damn mad at Daddy for "standing by his man," but most of the time I was crying because he had to go through that. And he *had* to do it, because Daddy is a loyal guy. He stuck by Clinton to the end, no matter how ugly the situation got, no matter how mad I got. One day a lady asked him, "Mr. Carville, one day your little girls are going to grow up. And they are going to find out what President Clinton did, and they may come to you and ask you how you could defend and associate yourself with such a man. My question to you, sir, is 'What will you tell them?'" Daddy took a deep breath and replied, "Ma'am, I will tell my girls that their daddy had a friend. And his friend did a bad thing. And what you do when you have a friend is you forgive him. And that's what I did. And I'm still proud to call him my friend."

A good question for you to ponder on loyalty is one Daddy was often asked at that ugly time. How loyal is too loyal? Are there no limits to loyalty? At what point does the loyal soldier turn into the lackey?

I believe loyalty ends when it ceases to be reciprocal. If you cannot count on someone as much as you know they can count on you, then you need to take an objective look at that relationship. Daddy is relentlessly objective and practical. His enduring loyalty to his friend was steeped in what he deemed to be a reliably reciprocal relationship. In time, he has proven to be correct.

Another time to take a loyalty check is when your loyalty enables or blinds you to a destructive behavior. I tend to be too loyal to staff I have personally hired. My gut check is rarely wrong. Once, in campaign crunch time, I hired a seemingly stellar administrative assistant: hardworking but gentle; attentive but never overbearing; tireless but never hyper; on top of everything, personal and professional.

One day I opened my own mail—a rare occurrence. My bank statement indicated sequential, unauthorized, *substantial* cash withdrawals. Then I opened my credit card statements, which all showed large charges, none of which I'd made. I turned to my perfect personal assistant for an explanation. I got no explanation but plenty of shock and outrage. I got furious assurances of immediate action; promises to scream at the bank and demand explanations from credit card representatives.

The rest of my staff gingerly suggested there weren't too many explanations for this money sieve. I vociferously, boisterously defended my perfect right-hand worker. I was loyal to my people. Well, it turned out that all that tireless perfection had been fueled by massive, regular infusions of cocaine—which continued to be underwritten by my bank accounts while I dithered in denial.

That's probably an extreme case of blinding loyalty, but a good example of what Daddy says is one of my more serious flaws: that I assume others will be loyal because I am loyal. He worries that that trait leaves me vulnerable and often disappointed in workplace situations.

I'm a bit tougher than Daddy's admonition suggests, but it is true that "I think like I think" (to use his terminology) when it comes to loyalty. He says I should "think like they think." Here's what I think *you* should think when it comes to loyalty: always be loyal yourself and presume the same in others. You may encounter disloyalty and it will surely hurt, but don't respond in kind. As Ma would say, "Don't sink to their level." Loyalty strengthens its giver and recipient alike. A deep sense of loyalty can help you overcome almost any bump in the road. Human endeavor is enhanced by loyalty. The disloyal may gain an advantage in some work situations, but their gains will be fleeting. Over time, and usually pretty quickly, the disloyal will show themselves to be losers. They will fail their institutions, their colleagues, and worst of all, themselves. It's okay to feel sorry for them, but get away from them as fast as a scalded dog.

When I was growing up, I used to bellow out in my best diva imitation, "People . . . people who need people are the luckiest people in the world . . ." (I still bellow this, especially wherever there's an open mike. I'm waiting for my big break!) When I was younger, I thought the song was lauding needy people. I don't like needy people. I don't mean the less fortunate among us, I mean those clingy, risk-averse, in-denial types; they feel like hot breath on my neck.

My appreciation for loyal friends and colleagues has intensified as I've aged, and now when I belt out "People," I'm paying tribute to the need to bond. Bonding cannot happen without loyalty. No loyalty, no bonding; nothing but loneliness. That's why loyalty isn't just a good workplace trait, it's a *necessary condition* of soul-mating. It's what distinguishes us from animals. (Except really great dogs. I highly recommend them if you need an emergency loyalty fix. They also can really keep secrets.)

I'm not worried about you guys. I don't see you two going to the dogs any time soon. You're already instinctively loyal to your friends and family. So when you bump up against detached, cynical, disloyal people, pity them and move on, *fast*. You'll always find loyal friends because you are loyal, and that makes you the luckiest people in the world!

Faithfully yours,
Mom

A Grand Old Flag

Dear Young Patriots,

Because I worked in the last two and current Republican administrations, I get all kinds of e-mails, calls, mail from every manner of political junkie, from the deeply sincere to the crackpots who can't live another minute without sharing their latest brainstorm. The polite ones start out, "I'm sure you will want to share this with President Bush," or "You need to tell Dick Cheney . . ." Others might begin, "Watching you makes me want to puke."

Apparently I come across as both earnest and crackpot (sometimes simultaneously) when it comes to politics, which makes me a magnet for the concerns of the politically active. And I love them all.

I've been crazy about politics for a long time now. There's a fine line between crazy about politics and a political crackpot. I've gone over the top a time or two but generally, to be an authentic political crackpot, you have to believe that conspiracies involving black helicopters are an integral part of politics.

Serious folks care deeply about and believe they can make a difference in the affairs of our country. Political junkies remain in a pretty much continuous state of agitation over the most minute political events, opining on every topic, whether or not they have any actual knowledge of said topic. At home I watch all the shout shows, throw stuff, and swear at the TV. (At twenty-five cents a cuss word, Matty is up to sixty-five dollars in her cursing-mom collection. Election years are jackpots for you guys.) We know that normal people (at least the kind of normal crazy people we are) can make a difference, because we have. And to tell you the truth, even crackpots can have a big impact. Check out Ross Perot and Ralph Nader.

There are all kinds of folks involved in politics, and that's a great achievement—a hallmark of our great system. No matter how wacky some might be, or how much you might hear me swear at them (or see them gag at me), the involved people are the true American patriots. There's only one kind of bad person in politics: the unpatriotic person who doesn't believe in, doesn't try to participate in, doesn't care about politics. Daddy tells a joke that always makes me sad: A pollster asks a guy, "What do you think is the worse thing about politics today, ignorance or apathy?" The guy answers, "Frankly, I don't know and I don't

care." More truth is said in jest, etc. (a big, big momism).
It's really pathetic how many lazy, ignorant, cynical U.S.
citizens there are. Actually, you can almost excuse lazy
and ignorant—that's a fairly common state for humans—
but there's no accounting for the cynics. You can't have
lived in this country, read more than two pages of history,
or considered for one minute the future and *not* be astounded, overwhelmed by the magnificence and miracle
of America: what it means to be an American and what
America means to the world.

Daddy and I made a pact before you guys were born
that we would not try to influence your political thinking.
Except for the occasional minor lapse on my part (like
marching around the kitchen with a poster, singing, "Dub-
a-yoo, Dub-a-yoo"), we keep to it. I try to answer your
questions about the news (even when I am yelling at it) ob-
jectively, without recourse to philosophical proselytizing;
sometimes I fail, but then if I'm in a real (rare) generous
mood, I will concede that there are two views on most topics (no need to elaborate on the one I don't agree with).
Daddy doesn't like for me to talk about politics at all, but
this is unrealistic when you live in a house where the parents are frequently either taking issue (loudly) with or
making fun (gleefully) of each other on almost any political subject. You want to know what we're yucking about
and you watch the news. He doesn't realize how well you
already think for yourselves. (Emma told me to tell the

vice president that Arafat needs a time-out; Matty made me send a letter to Poppy Bush pleading for the Washington sniper not to get the death penalty.)

I confess it's hard to resist the temptation to do a little conservative evangelizing, and it's not just because I want to honor the pact that I back off. It's been my observation that people embrace their political grounding with deeper conviction if they come to it on their own.

Don't ever feel like you have to choose between Daddy and me or, more important, take up any political opinion out of peer pressure or because it's trendy. *Think for yourself. Speak for yourself.* What Daddy and I *do* agree on is that even though we won't force-feed you our respective philosophies, we will insist on your own good citizenship.

Here are a few basics on citizenship. This country is great because its people are. Progress is not an accident. The democracy and freedom and opportunities we enjoy are the product of a belief system put to the test many times over. Our country has never failed to defend our values and to advance them if we need to, whether to ensure our system or help others secure their own freedom. We will only ever be as good as our citizens keep us. Our progress is enhanced by greater participation.

The bare minimum of good citizenship is participation through voting. It's best if you are an *informed* voter, but where I come from, we were taught to "vote early and often" for the Daley family, and where Daddy comes from, a very powerful governor was so assured of loyal voters he once said, "The only way I'll lose is if I get caught sleeping with a live boy or a dead girl." So I have a soft spot for party-line voting because the Daley family made Chicago grand *and* neighborly and Edwin Edwards made politics amusing.

I'm a straight-ticket GOP voter—which is sometimes considered unsophisticated. Voting for one party over another isn't wrong; not voting at all is wrong.

The next level of good citizenship is actually knowing what you believe in and why. Margaret Thatcher said, "Standing in the middle of the road is very dangerous; you get knocked down by traffic from both sides." Picking a side requires some study, thought, data assessment— activities that are not a given for many political activists today. People think I'm joking when I say I was raised a liberal and became a conservative when I started thinking and reading and actually connecting policies to their results. But, lest it appear I am violating the No-Political-Influencing Parent Pact, I'm only giving you the guidebook, not the destination. Study, think, observe reality, and come to your own conclusions.

The next step up the ladder of good citizenship is acting on your belief system beyond just voting. Your parents' political activism is a tad more involved than the average citizen participation, but you don't have to work on campaigns or in the White House to be a political activist. Any community or neighborhood service counts. Writing to your elected representatives counts. Calling City Hall counts. Letters to the editor, organizing for a cause, volunteering on a campaign at any level, contributing money to a candidate counts.

To be a good citizen, you must use your voice. Anyone who tells you it doesn't matter—that one person can't make a difference, that the system is corrupt—is a moron. I'm not saying it's easy or that there aren't corrupt losers in it, but as Winston Churchill said, "Democracy is the worst system devised by the wit of man, except for all the others."

We're not just talking about a political system here. This land of the free and home of the brave is the pinnacle of human progress, to my mind. I was raised a patriot by the sons and daughters of immigrants to whom freedom was no abstract concept. There were no cynics on those packed boats coming to America. My grandpa, who had very little English, would bellow out "The Halls of Montezuma" and cry at every family gathering. I get choked up when we sing "The Star-Spangled Banner" at baseball games.

Our country is strong because our people are patriots. Patriotism is participation, not holding to a political party or point of view. Patriots participate. They debate. They give of themselves for their country.

Your community and school suffered losses on 9/11, so

you two have seen close up what it means to give for your country. This past Christmas, Matty's third-grade teacher, Mrs. Wehrey, was overjoyed because her husband got to come home from Baghdad just a few days after his fellow soldiers captured Saddam Hussein. Mrs. Wehrey brought her husband to Matty's class party to surprise you kids. Well, the biggest treat was for the parents. We were all so bowled over—tingly happy for Mrs. Wehrey, who had been the most engaged teacher all fall even though she was so very worried. But even more goose-bump-producing was our pride in Captain Wehrey. We all crowded around and kept shaking his hand and hugging her and thanking him.

I hope we conveyed our pride in Captain Wehrey (he seemed slightly embarrassed with all the fuss), but I didn't hear anyone really able to express the profound sense of patriotism we shared in his sacrifice. That's how I feel now. I cannot *tell* you what it means to be an American, how it feels to say "I am an American," to put up the big flag in our front yard, to understand how free people can change the course of history and lift up whole nations from oppression. You will study these things and we'll make sure you'll see them for yourself. We are in the midst of a struggle between civilization and barbarism, between going forward or falling backward, between liberty and tyranny.

The world has been at such a crossroad before. America has always taken the path to freedom. In the greatest struggles, America has led the way, made that path possible. The millions of liberated souls do not take their freedom for granted or think it came by accident. I wonder what an Eastern European father or Afghani mother would say to the cynic who believes you can't make a difference.

Closer to home, America's support of and belief in personal liberty has accelerated progress undreamed of even when I was your age, progress in medicine, mobility, communication, technology, equal opportunity, and security.

I happen to believe that the political philosophy that favors the individual, that provides an environment of maximum freedom, will produce the greatest good for the community at large. Others believe in a different road, but they want to get to the same place. Think of it as a big fight over directions. The point is, gaining freedom, maintaining freedom, using freedom are all the result of individual effort or the concerted action of many individuals brought together by the same values. You are blessed to live in this epicenter of freedom and you have a responsibility to keep it strong and pass it on.

God bless America,
Mom

P.S. Vote early and often!

GLOBE-TROTTING

Dear Fellow Travelers,

After lunch at a breezy hilltop café, you both beelined to one of the ice-cream stands perched on every Italian street corner. I said, *"Uno"*; you pointed to chocolate. Yet another incredibly beautiful Italian girl handed you the dish of almost-black-it's-so-chocolate, which Matty informed us has twice the fat and sugar of American ice cream. "How did you know that?" I asked, pretty impressed. "TV," you retorted, naming the source of all your best information. I tried to impress you by chirping to the beautiful girl, *"Due gelato."* She handed me another ice cream. *"No, no, gelato."* She handed me a third dish. Exasperated, feeling like an especially ugly American, I paid, clueless as to what they cost or whether I got the correct change back. Huffily, I flipped to my in-flight Italian instruction book to figure out why I couldn't get the second spoon I had so clearly requested. *Due gelato, due gelato.* Two ice creams. Spoon is *cucchiaio,* not even close. Matty gave me that look. "I could've told you *gelato* means ice cream. Saw it on TV."

Growing up outside Chicago, I'd never traveled beyond Little Paw Paw, Michigan, where we went on a family vacation, until I was well into my twenties. I'd never been anywhere that had even a hint of historical interest until I moved to Washington for my first Republican Party job at age twenty-seven.

Matty had 31,000 frequent flyer miles before she was three months old; among Emma's first complete sentences was "Return your seats to their upright and locked positions." You've been to almost every major city in the country; should I be worried that your personal favorite is Las Vegas?

I am a knee-jerk "nothing is better than the USA" booster. I love our country's natural beauty and our hard-fought origin; I love our industries and industriousness; I love our fast thinkers and fast food. I love that we are at once a self-confident and a self-conscious country.

I cannot remember when I first started feeling blessed to be born in America; I only know that it remains a regular thought. Daddy says if he had been born somewhere else, he'd be a taxi driver at best. Maybe there's another place where an Irish-Croatian kid like me with a mediocre education can go from cutting hair in an East Chicago beauty school to cutting up in the Oval Office, but I don't know where that is.

I loved where I grew up; to this day I love the smell and sounds of heavy industry and assembly lines (the few that are left). In reality, it was damn stinky and truly a blight on the landscape, but I didn't know that then. I adored my home but couldn't wait to see the rest of the country. I cut out pictures from *National Geographic* and wallpapered my bedroom with them. But I had no idea how much beauty and man-made mastery was out there.

My early national political jobs all required traveling, traversing the country from coast to coast. The first time I saw New York City—from the driver's seat of my '79 Chevy jalopy—it took my breath away. I gaped at the magnificence of the George Washington Bridge, crowned with lights, a gateway to the astounding, mind-boggling, skyscraping mountains of aggressive American achievement. (I still get pumped going to NYC.)

Coming from the Midwest, I thought I had a sense of space until my first trip west, to the Badlands, the peaks of the Teton Mountains (which really are purple mountain majesties), canyons, deserts, endless sky. As incredible as the scenery is, I found myself imagining the treks of Lewis and Clark (promise me you'll read Stephen Ambrose) and of the pioneers, the Mormons, the gold diggers, farmers, woodsmen, every manner of entrepreneur (and charlatan) who pushed through this astounding beauty and constant danger. What did they think when they first laid eyes on this large land? What kept them going through the daunting terrain?

I cannot go anywhere in the country without mentally time-traveling back to the first Americans to see and settle the land. You will learn the link between geography and destiny, but you must *experience* it. You must also witness the unique American ingenuity of our cities (promise me you'll read Ayn Rand).

Shamefully, we rarely take advantage of the glorious city we live in, Washington, D.C. Our nation's capital is truly one of the world's great cities. Its setting, history, art, and neighborhoods demand exploration. Its architecture is fascinating for its self-conscious copycatting of Europe. And it's right across the river from the quintessentially American architecture of Old Town, Virginia, where we can walk through our history from George Washington's church to Robert E. Lee's mansion.

My two other faves are Chicago and New Orleans, total opposites and each a unique window on our colorful history. Common to both is one of our country's greatest assets, our immigrant population. Chicago speaks of dozens of families and neighbors and heritages. Folks who set out with clarity of purpose—a better life—link us to much that was special in their birth homes. These immigrants and their offspring are especially proud Americans because they don't take our greatness for granted. And we are better Americans to have access through them to their unique heritages. (My all-time favorite campaign events are the food festivals in the ethnic neighborhoods.) I'll tell you something strange and wonderful. Whenever my travels have taken me to (now democratic) Eastern Europe, I feel right at home!

As much as I'm a pathologically patriotic travel agent for America, I must admit that the world is wondrous, remarkable, unimaginable, and indescribable. You must travel beyond our borders—a lot, all over. You have little appreciation for it now, but traveling is the most broadening experience you can undertake. Exposure to other places and peoples is simultaneously expanding and humbling, like making out constellations for the first time. You connect your own time and place with a brand-new, eye-popping perspective that comes from experiencing the past and current achievements of other cultures.

Daddy and I love to experience different cultures; we're suckers for everything from architecture and art to customs and cuisine. *Oohing* and *aahing* across the expansive lavender patches of southern France or slobbering through six courses of fresh Tuscan fare washed down with wine from the back yard, we always raise a glass to *"la dolce vita."*

"The good life" of old Europe was an interesting discovery: no place on earth moves at the pace of America. We've found that to be true not just in Europe but in South and Central America, Asian countries, Arab states. It's not just that we're faster; we move with a greater sense of purpose. Our goal is the *destination*. In other countries I've visited, the *journey* sets the pace. Our sense of purposeful hurry can be off-putting to other cultures, but they also envy what that uniquely American trait has produced: *America*. You can always spot newly arrived Americans abroad just by their twitchiness. It takes a while to recalibrate your rhythms. Meetings abroad ramble meaninglessly, but meals mean business. Naps and teas are cultural mandates.

You can't appreciate the appeal of other places until you adjust your metabolic rate. Once you do, truly exotic worlds emerge: proud histories that reach back to antiquity, cultures stopped in time by oppression or just plain bad government, unparalleled opulence, mortifying poverty.

Just as in America, I can never travel abroad without zeroing in on how countries and cultures developed the way they did. Americans tend to think in compressed time frames since our progress has been so speedy. To trace back the growth of Christianity or any organized global religion—our moral history—by actually touching a sacred place from a distant time always overwhelms my short American attention span. San Clemente in Rome is layer upon layer of worship centers built on top of each other since pagan days! This summer we saw a horse-race pageant called the Palio in Siena that dates back seven hundred years, practiced exactly the same way by participants clad in precise replicas of contemporary fashions, including hairdos! (You girls were focused on the boys' Prince Valiant haircuts; our traveling buddy, Miss Ollie, and I zoomed in on their leotards!)

Traveling to these timeless places will make you more diligent about preserving your country's own physical and cultural history. If I had my druthers, I would make you study and travel abroad before you get into real life. Since I suppose I have to let you have some say in your adult lives, while you're still mine totally, I'm gonna make *sure* you see beyond your shores.

Today at sunset we climbed through a medieval hill town overlooking a postcard-perfect sweep of rosemary-covered fields, to a park square where old people sat chatting and practicing soon-to-be-lost handicrafts—crocheting linens, hammering copper, weaving baskets and chairs, throwing pots, cobbling shoes, spinning yarn—all while ancient church bells clanged from every direction. You were your perpetually nonchalant selves until you discovered yet another ice-cream stand. This time I *did* impress you when my *"Due gelato"* actually produced two ice creams!

Ti amo,
Mama

TEACH YOUR
CHILDREN WELL

Dear Budding Big Brains,

We're gonna have a love/hate struggle with your educations. You're gonna hate my endlessly bugging you about learning while you're growing up and love me for it when you're grown. I was way too cavalier with my own formal education—despite my mom and dad's repeated warning, "You'll never have this opportunity again." My parents never had a chance to just go to school, to take full advantage of a learning environment. They were always working or taking care of family.

They gave me that opportunity and I blew it. Mostly I took the bare minimum of courses to graduate and crammed the night before exams to get good grades. I wish I had studied more subjects simply because I enjoyed them, even if they were off the beaten path or impractical.

As a geezer, I now realize that the role seemingly inessential courses played in captivating and sparking my imagination made them the most valuable, fulfilling ones of all. I'll be on you like white on rice about your education—not about getting the best grades but about getting the most out of your formal learning years and acquiring a real appreciation and desire for lifetime learning.

Our education system may be flawed, but it produces extraordinary creators, entrepreneurs, humane and progressive leaders. Sure, we can always make advances and improvements, but *if you want a good education in this country, you can get one.* The biggest impediment to a solid education isn't the problems with our system, it's attitude. So let's start there.

Too many of my generation had the wrong attitude about education, which left us less educated than we should be. We didn't appreciate the ready availability of it; so many women and minorities around the globe are denied access even today. When education opened up in this country, prejudices didn't close down. I'm not talking about the hurtful prejudice minorities faced; I mean cultural predispositions. When Ma asked her dad if she could go to nursing school, he said, "No way." She was "just gonna get married and have kids." She gave up that dream, but when we kids were in school, she went to beauty school. Despite the fact that she was a frighteningly bad hairdresser, she graduated at the top of her class and ended up running the school business. She was so eager to learn, she never took any opportunity for education for granted.

Even for white men, education wasn't as available for my parents' generation as it is today. Poppy would never have gotten his mechanical engineering degree without the GI Bill. My generation, even us blue-collar kids, considered a good education our birthright, but we appreciated it less.

You were absolutely shocked to learn that little girls in Afghanistan weren't allowed to go to school. You'd be equally horrified to know how many schools around the world are really inadequate. So appreciate that you even have access to education, not to mention good schools.

A lot of people also need an attitude adjustment about the point of education. Learning shouldn't be just a means to riches. Learning is enriching in and of itself. I truly believe in the saying "Do what you love, the money will follow." Pursuing a field just to make money, you might get an education, but you won't *learn* anything. You'll just "game the system" to graduate.

So many people choose a career in law just for big bucks, and it does pay. But I know more miserable lawyers who hated law school than I can count. (These are never the ones you want to represent you!) Law school was my worst school experience. I went to "get a good job"; my happiest day was when I dropped out to take a job I loved (campaigning for Reagan-Bush '84). The law is fascinating; I love studying it as it pertains to public policy and politics, but when I was studying it to make money, I learned nothing, remembered nothing, and developed a teeth-grinding habit I have to this day! Your cousin Rich, who graduated at the top of his Georgetown Law School class, hated practicing law just to make money. He gave up the good life to go after the bad guys. He loves being a prosecutor for a fraction of his former salary. I hope you'll appreciate not just the opportunity to learn but the beauty of knowledge for knowledge's sake.

Another self-imposed limitation on learning is thinking that being smart is uncool. I always had a gravitational pull to smart kids, especially the dorks! Dorks are usually so labeled by "cool kids" who have to put someone else down to keep themselves up. True cool kids accept and appreciate everyone for his or her unique gifts.

Sometimes kids get labeled dorks just for being different. I promise you this: *everyone* is different. Everyone learns differently. Our education system took a quantum leap forward when it incorporated this reality into teaching. When Daddy and I were in school, we were all taught the same way. If you didn't learn that way, it was easy to get left behind. Now teachers teach to each kid's unique receptivity. Good teachers can get through to any kid on any subject. I've learned so much about this subject from Aunt Renie, who teaches students with learning disabilities. I'm not a big fan of PC language, but whoever invented the term "differently abled" got it right when it comes to learning. We're *all* special needs in one way or another. We *all* benefit from learning in a way that speaks to our strengths and minimizes our deficiencies. How we learn has absolutely nothing to do with how smart we are. If you're passionate about learning something and a particular teaching method isn't helping you, keep at it; find the teacher and approach that works for you.

By the way, IQ—intelligence quotient—is but one measurement of intelligence. The older I get, the more I see that it's probably not the best predictor of success or productivity or happiness. I know a lot of really stupid smart people. They're smart as a whip with facts and dumb as a post with people. Since we live in a world with facts *and* people, you need to work on your EI—emotional intelligence—as much as your IQ.

Don't limit your education to book learning. Study people. Talk to them, especially people of varied backgrounds. My grandma from Croatia, who never had a formal education, was my window on the world. To this day, my point of reference for Europe and twentieth-century global politics is her perspective, which comes from her experience in a Communist country. Talk and listen to people who disagree with you. You can get rigor mortis of the brain if you only talk with people who agree with you.

To really get the most out of your education, understand that your opportunities for learning extend way beyond the classroom. Travel; enroll in internships and extracurricular and community activities; go to museums, concerts, movies, plays; work, at *any* work. (I learned more from waitressing and bartending—and got paid more—than I did cramming for classes.) Take classes that won't lead to anything—acting, singing, any instrument, painting, bowling. Expand your horizons. My mother and I had a riot in ceramics. I shouldn't say that class didn't lead to anything: we must have made a hundred ugly coffee mugs! Ma took oil painting—at which she displayed a talent only marginally better than her horrific hairdressing—but it engaged and enriched her. My parents made me take accordion lessons (it was an ethnic thing). You want to talk *dork!* Maybe so, but to this day, accordion music takes me away. Remember that street accordionist at the outdoor café in Siena? You guys laughed when I got all choked up, but appreciating music by knowing how it happens is an unparalleled experience. Maybe music or art won't be what turns you on; you'll be more likely to find out what cranks your chain if you explore more subjects, in and out of a formal setting.

It's also terrific good fun to learn with someone. When Daddy and I set out to learn about something together (wine, watchmaking, history), he always brings a perspective I wouldn't have thought of. And he inspires me to dig deeper on my end by his relentless (hyper!) questioning.

Learning is lifelong. Some adults love to lament, "If I knew then what I know now . . ." I operate on the principle, "What can I learn next?" Don't worry about what you didn't get then, just go get it now. My dad got his MBA when he was fifty-one. My mom took an economics class the summer before she died. And even though the mention of it is freaking you guys out, I *am* gonna take singing lessons someday.

You have opportunities I could only dream of at your age, opportunities that most of the world, even in this age, cannot begin to dream of. Daddy and I are so excited for you, excited about what you will do with those opportunities—for yourself and this world. We both want you to know that the measure of a good education (or successful life) isn't winning a Nobel or finding a cure for cancer. It's discovering the world, finding what you love, and finding yourself along the way.

By the way, you two have taught us way more than anything else has, and the most valuable of all things,

Love,
Your Teacher and Student,
Mom

P.S. You still better bring home decent report cards.

WHY DID THE COW
CROSS THE ROAD?

Dear Born Comedians,

I knew when I first saw you totally engrossed in *I Love Lucy* that Daddy and I had passed on a trait we share and relish: the humor gene. Our family will laugh at anything. We actually study jokes. Our best bud Jon Macks, who writes jokes for Jay Leno and textbooks on comedy, has tried to teach Daddy and me how to make up our own jokes, but alas, we only have the ear, not the voice.

Humor is not just fun, it's a potent defense mechanism—which you have already mastered. God, it's annoying when I'm getting ready to snarl at you and one of you blasts back with "Knock, knock!" I really, really try to resist, but my mouth automatically forms the words, "Who's there?" For the hundredth time: "A little boy who can't reach the door bell." *Aarrggghhh . . . hahahahaha.*

Daddy is a born raconteur; he can really tell a story.

Unfortunately, he can also really tell (and loves to tell) bodily function jokes. Actually, he *performs* bodily functions *as* jokes. These are so lame that I laugh at how goofy he is, which only encourages him.

Your gene pool is flooded with jokesters; most of our nonblood relatives and best friends are wack jobs too. Daddy's sisters and Miss Ollie have introduced me to a whole new genre of jokes. Cajuns, or as they call themselves, "coon-asses," must have a million of these joke stories. I have never heard the same one twice in twelve years! I cannot resist sharing a sampling with you. Most of the Cajun jokes are not for kids, but Miss Ollie sent some you can use. You have to tell them in that inimitable accent you hear at gatherings of Daddy's kin.

THE BASIC WIFE SETUP

Boudreaux came up to Thibodeaux and said: "Thibodeaux, I've got some good news and some bad news." Thibodeaux says, "What be the bad news?" Boudreaux replies: "Your wife, Marie, she be found in the bayou. She done pass away." Thibodeaux: "Oh my God, that is purtty bad. What be the good news?" Boudreaux: "Well, when we found her, she had over a dozen crab on her, so in another hour we gonna make another run!"

The Basic Husband Setup

Boudreaux was on his last dying breath. He was upstairs in the waterbed and was about to slip out of this world when he smelled it.

The most wonderful smell. Brownies, baking in the oven downstairs.

He struggled out of the waterbed. He could not stand up so he crawled over to the stairway and rolled down the stairs. He crawled into the kitchen and pulled himself up to the counter where the brownies were cooling on the rack. He took one and put it to his mouth. Aw, that wonderful smell, that wonderful taste.

Marie walked up behind him and said, "Shame on you, Boudreaux. Those brownies are for after the funeral."

(You might need a couple of Bud Lights to get the full appreciation of coon-ass jokes.)

Humor is no laughing matter. (See why no one laughs at me?) Humor is seriously high-order thinking, not just entertainment. It also serves as a people-meter. My nonscientific personal poll shows it's hard to deal with people who can't tell a joke or get a joke. There's something more than the appreciation of a good punchline that's missing in the humor-impaired. These unfortunates take themselves too seriously, which makes them really boring, which is not a place or space you want to spend a lot of time in.

Humor is a profound elixir, practically a panacea. It's the gift that keeps on giving. You can laugh at the same joke for years. (Okay, maybe that's just us.) It's portable and inexpensive and ingratiating. Humor breaks the ice and soothes the soul. It connects and bonds you to like-minded weirdos—a term of endearment, in my book.

Of all the advice in these letters, here is the most serious: Don't be.

Take my wife, please,

Mom

P.S. Because she wanted to go to the *mooooo*vies.

IT'S MY PARTY AND I'LL CRY IF I WANT TO

Dear Future Crybabies!

Today was the day before the actual first day of school—the day you found your classrooms and saw who your new teachers were. Despite the brevity of the event, I still managed to soak two tissues. Matty took this common occurrence in stride; Emma was mortified. I feel Emma's pain (as we Republicans *love* to say; you just had to be there). I was embarrassed myself, but I *always* cry at school events. I suspect the other mothers think this is slightly over the top. During Spotlight on Authors, when the students in Matty's class each read aloud for all the parents the stories they'd taken the entire year to write, one mother asked me, was she mistaken or did I start crying *before* Matty took the stage?

I cry because I'm simply overwhelmed: overwhelmed by love, pride, even fear. (You're out of my sight at school!

What if you were abducted by aliens? I'm not making this up; when Matty was a newborn, I actually had an escape plan for alien invasion. I hardly believe it myself, but it was a serious plan. Please see my letter on raging hormones!) Overwhelmed that you are your own, unguided, individual, unique *selves*, separate little people. I am thunderbolted by the miracle of your existence. Not just the miracle of birth, but the miracle of your beings, your distinct humanness. I never thought I could marvel as much as I did when you were infants, but if anything, my awe has intensified as I watch you take shape, both your growing bodies and, even more mesmerizing and mystifying, your flowering souls.

If you guys are embarrassed by my crying, look at what I just wrote. It's a miracle I'm not in a body bag, the way I fall apart thinking about how wonderful you are. Cut me some slack!

Sometimes, I do wish I could control the way I always burst out crying over everything you do. It grosses you guys out, it makes your teachers feel awkward, and worst of all, it always gives Daddy a chuckle. He loves when I bust up; he thinks it's so "girly." Daddy loves girly-girls.

Crying *is* a girly-girl thing, yet another of our special gifts. Yet another intrinsic female strength the man-imitating feminists wrongly rejected.

Crying is *not* a weakness. Whining is a weakness; it's my

personal pet peeve. Crying is never whiny. Crying is cathartic and cleansing, no matter what the cause: great or tragic events, extreme anxiety or relief, exhilaration or grief, a goober love fest or screeching fight, button-busting accomplishments or humiliating failures.

Have you broken the code yet? People who live life with the fullest commitment tend to cry a lot. Just because you have deep emotional reactions to life doesn't mean you're an emotional basket case. It could mean you pull away from mediocrity and banality, safety, boredom. You gravitate to bigger situations and you experience them fully, for better or for worse.

Crying is a healthy expression of deep emotions. I don't like or trust people who don't or can't cry. You can't reach those people because they haven't reached themselves. Emotionally healthy people aren't afraid of their emotions.

Crying can also help you stay emotionally stable when it serves as a leading indicator. If you ever find yourself crying for no reason, it's because you've got a problem—a hard problem, one you don't want to deal with. Crying is surely a healthier indicator of denial than say, drinking, drugging, or ax-murdering.

I keep telling you that you can never solve any problem until you identify it. And now I'm telling you, there are going to be problems for which there is no solution *but* crying. Those tears will be a tonic. Some life events are so unfair, inexplicable, unbearable that the only response and relief is crying, or so maddening you *have* to cry before you can respond.

Right now all crying bothers you. As an involuntary product of men-wannabe feminism, I cry less when I'm upset (except during obvious tragedies, and we've had many this year) than when I'm ecstatic. The tough-chicks-don't-cry brainwashing worked on me. Instead of having a good clear-the-decks cry, I get extremely foul-tempered and counterproductive, snappy and dismissive. I wish there was a cry-therapy class for this, a no-tears deprogramming center.

Some life events are so glorious that there are no adequate words for them, just tears of joy; our family is big on tears of joy. This not only embarrasses you guys but also scares you, like when Daddy surprised me by flying in my dad and Grandma Barb for our tenth wedding anniversary. My dad—your Poppy—and I clung, clutched, and cried for so long that you guys started whimpering, you were so scared. Had something awful happened? Had we lost it completely? Just the opposite: we *had* it completely, and there was nothing—*nothing*—my father or I could say to each other at that moment to express our deep love.

You can't beat tears of joy: the ones that spurt out over holidays, movies and plays, music, Matty's jokes, Emma's singing, weddings, elections (I always cry when I vote), new babies, "The Star-Spangled Banner." You guys had so much fun making fun of me in Italy for weeping over the extraordinary art. When Daddy and I were dating, I almost gave him a heart attack when I burst out crying over a Botticelli in Venice. Later I *think* I saw him tear up over the Berninis in Rome. I *know* I've seen him get soggy over Hank Williams!

We should keep a crying catalogue. I guarantee you, any event worth remembering will include tears.

Given the multiple benefits of crying and the hazards of "holding it in" (not to mention the literal chemical necessity of tears; check out your biology books), it's profoundly stupid that, as a culture, we Americans have denigrated crying as a weakness. That women can cry better is just another sign of our superiority.

So go ahead and cry when you have to and when you want to, but follow the rules of the road. Rule #1: No fake crying to get what you want. This is tough to avoid because men are suckers for it. Parents will do anything to stop it. But it's manipulative and wrong, and it gives crying a bad name. Rule #2: Hormonally induced crying usually means nothing. Just go with it. It's better than a box of Godivas or half a dozen new Bruno Maglis. Rule #3: Never trust men who cannot cry; never trust men who can cry on command. (The same thing goes for quivering lips and blinking back tears.) As a corollary, never, *ever* make fun of a boy or man who cries. And rule #4: If your love interest doesn't move you to tears either of joy or fits, you're not in love.

Now you know why you so often reduce me to tears, from stuttering sniffles to full-on wailing, and why I laugh till I cry with Aunt Renie or Aunt Maria, and why Daddy loses it when *you* cry. Crying connects us. You understand why Daddy and I cry so much over Uncle Bill and Uncle Stevie. Why I wanted to cry for you when you lost your first and dearest caregiver, Nee-Nee. Why Maria and I just busted out together when we first saw our new houses wiped out by the flood. Crying comforts us.

So, girls, crying is a good thing. Stock up on that waterproof mascara. And I pray you'll have someone in your lives who makes you cry tears of joy as much as you do me.

XOXO,
Mom

YOU ARE SO BEAUTIFUL

Dear Lovelies,

Audrey Hepburn wrote this when asked to share her "beauty tips." (The original author was one Samuel Levenson, whose swan neck wasn't nearly so famous.)

For attractive lips, speak words of kindness.

For lovely eyes, seek out the good in people.

For a slim figure, share your food with the hungry.

For beautiful hair, let a child run his/her fingers through it once a day.

For poise, walk with the knowledge that you never walk alone.

People, even more than things, have to be restored, renewed, revived, reclaimed, and redeemed; never throw out anyone.

> Remember, if you ever need a helping hand, you
>   will find one at the end of each of your arms.
> As you grow older, you will discover that you have
>   two hands; one for helping yourself, and the
>   other for helping others.

Whenever I took some beauty question to Ma—the owner of one of Don Roberts' Beauty Schools for many years (she went to school there, taught for years, and then bought one for herself) and therefore the ultimate arbiter of how to look good—she always gave me the same response, her number-one rule on beauty: "It's better to be beautiful on the inside than the outside." If I pressed her, she'd pass along some dos and don'ts. Don't shave your legs; if you start too soon, your calves will feel like your father's chin. Do shave your armpits, if you don't, you'll smell like roadkill. Believe it or not, hairy armpits were in fashion for a while. Ma was vigorously welcoming of new fashion trends (unless they were hygienically challenged, like long armpit hair) and surprisingly tolerant of even the most counterproductive, for example, bralessness. She clucked when my girlfriends and I went out bouncing and swinging free but only admonished, "You'll regret this when your birdies are sitting on your belly button." Oh, did I roll my eyes at that when I was fourteen! By forty I was ordering heavy-duty, cast-iron underwires from New

York, just to get halfway back up from belly button terri-
tory! You know how I always set off the metal detector at
airports? That's because I've got a tool box full of metal
propping me up, proving once again, listen to your
mother!

Actually, I personally didn't go braless for long in my
teens because that fashion madness was more of a political
than sartorial statement. Bra burning was a symbol of card-
carrying feminism, a shortsighted statement from our
would-be liberators. Another truly insane dictum was the
absolute proscription against makeup. Since cavewoman
days, down through the ages, women of all classes and colors have been painting their faces to ensnare and lord it
over their easily manipulated male counterparts; since we
could not get equality, the goal here was to get attention
for our "issues." For millennia, the female of the species
used and enhanced her appearance to get what she needed
from the male of the species, from offspring to protection
to riches to love. Feminists in my day believed fervently
that a woman using her looks was perpetuating an oppres-
sive patriarchy. This view disregarded the laws of nature:
all species use their looks to attract what they need. (In
most of the animal world, it's the male that puffs up.) Plus,
by nature, females like to get pretty. So the feminists es-
chewed the laws of nature to change the laws of man. The
battle gear of the feminist high priestesses leading the

charge for that promised land of female superiority was vulnerable, bouncing breasts; uncamouflaged faces; and gross, hairy pits and legs. Oh yeah, deodorant was verboten, basically allowing men to detect by olfactory means our assault so they could escape before they had to look at us. Maybe it was an effective political strategy: "Please, we'll do anything, just put on some lipstick and Secret!"

Most southern women never got anywhere near such political nonsense, because they've been controlling their men since our founding and were and remain the most beautiful women on earth in every and all circumstances. (As your father never neglects to remind me whenever he sees one, especially when one jauntily jogs by. To which I always respond, "If God meant for me to work out fully made up and coiffed, he wouldn't have created sweat, I mean spritz." Girls don't sweat, we glow. If we're really working it hard, we spritz.)

I include this little piece of history here because it was all going on as I approached my I-want-to-be-pretty years. (I still do want to be pretty, but then and now, to your father's constant bewilderment, I would much, much, much rather be smart, but we'll get to that later.) From the beginning I was barraged with double-barreled beauty bashing. Pleasing Ma meant forsaking outer for inner beauty. Political correctness meant beauty was bad. The more my social consciousness was raised, the worse I looked. Ma quickly intervened: I didn't have to look like a dog to do good. I could be political *and* pretty—well, as pretty as I could get. Ma's number-two rule on beauty was "You got to do the best you can with what you got." Let me underscore the operative concept here: what *you* got. Not what magazine covers, movie stars, music mavens, or even your best girlfriends got.

In my day everyone wanted to be Twiggy—a ninety-nine-pound blonde with big blue eyes who was never seen without a miniskirt. This was tough for me—a big, sturdy, squinty, brown-eyed, mousy brunette who wouldn't be caught dead with an exposed thigh. Nonetheless, I would position myself at the bathroom mirror while my (beautiful, blue-eyed, china-doll-skinned, 115-pound, redheaded) mom would transform me. Not with her voluminous expertise in makeup or hair, but with her absolute, irrevocable conviction that I was, on all the earth, in all of history, the *single most beautiful girl God ever created.* She never saw pores you could drive a Humvee through or hair so wispy someone breathing nearby could destroy any do. She saw a Rapunzel with marble-sculpted skin, and more important, she made me see. To this day, on my worst day, I stand at the mirror, take a deep breath, and say to myself, "I *will* do the best I can with what I got."

Happily, you two gorgeous girls have got much more

to work with, but here are some time-honored beauty tips from the inner sanctum of female secrets.

Tip #1: Anyone can look good, but no one looks good when she feels bad. If you're not feeling well or thinking straight, it will show. If you feel good, you'll look good; if you look good, you'll feel good. Easier-said-than-done advice here: Eat right, sleep tight, exercise every day. This is a package deal. You will eat, sleep, and exercise better if you do all three conscientiously. Each enhances your metabolic rate; together they can keep you "in the zone," energetic and thinking straight.

No matter how many books there are—and there are thousands on dieting and exercising—there is no single best way for everyone. You have to figure out what foods satisfy your appetite, how much sleep leaves you rested, and which exercises crank you up. My best advice here is moderation. As in all of life, don't let perfection be the enemy of good.

Let's start with dieting. Here are just a few of the diets we did when we were teens in the Twiggy era:

(a) The professional diets: all protein or all carbs; no protein or no carbs. My version of all-protein: nothing but canned corn beef. Problems: fatigue, bad breath, and yellow hands. My version of all carbs: nothing but baby food. Problems: bleeding gums, baby diarrhea.

(b) The homemade diets: These consisted of eating

only one thing to eliminate temptation. You could eat as much of whatever the one thing was, but *only* that one thing. The greatest hits here were grapefruit, cottage cheese, yogurt, apples, and brown rice. As you might imagine, those got boring fast, so we got more inventive.

(c) The as-much-as-you-want-but-only-creative-foods diets: These included banana milkshakes, brownies, Sugar Babies, Sara Lee cheesecakes, cheese popcorn, and our most memorable—Bazooka bubblegum. In college, we invented a variation on the brownies-only diet: brownies and beer. These diets were less boring, but they did produce an unwanted side effect— massive zits.

One time in high school, I went for eleven days consuming nothing but water. Once, in college, I went a week on pretzels and wine. On my first campaign, I went for months on Diet Coke and Peanut M&Ms.

The only thing these diets had in common is that they all produced the same outcome: weight gain.

I am now the weight I was in seventh grade and have been for over twenty years. My secret diet? No diet.

I eat what I want when I'm hungry but just enough to fill me up. I don't avoid all bad foods, but I do understand I'm not going to feel as good having a meal of potato chips and dip as I do having apples and peanut butter. It's taken me a while to figure it out, but I finally get it: if you eat poorly, you'll sleep poorly, and you'll be too beat to exercise well, which means you'll eat poorly and sleep poorly and round and round.

Add to your triad of good food, sleep, and exercise plenty of water and a daily vitamin. (If you're not tinkling every hour, you're not drinking enough water.) Daily prayer/meditation/reflection rounds off a good regimen.

If you aim for good health, you'll get good looks.

A note on exercise: Daddy and I work and work out in a regimented way. My dad was a regular gym-goer, so it's in my DNA. But here's what I've figured out on my own. First, regimens are easier with a friend. I only get up and out at 6 AM to sweat and grunt with Aunt Maria because we laugh so hard at each other's efforts to get into Trainer Trish's yoga contortions. Second, you don't need professional weights, a fancy workout room, or ill-fitting Spandex to exercise. Just move. Squeeze. Breathe. Stretch. You can do this anywhere, anytime. God created mobile phones so we could walk briskly while talking. Suck in your gut whenever you're doing anything. Squeeze your glutes during boring meetings. Keep everyday items on the highest shelves so you have to stre-e-e-etch for them. Take stairs two or three at a time to work your quads and hams. Lower yourself slowly into the tub to work your triceps. Do curls with tomato sauce cans for your biceps. Breathe in through your nose, out through your mouth.

For cardio, dance and sing while cleaning your house. (Someday you will *have* to clean at least your *room!*)

Tip #2: Be yourself. Accentuate the positive. Accept the negative. Appreciate the total package as uniquely you.

I've never known any girl who bypassed the "I wish I had" phase. If you're a blonde, you wish you were a red-head. If your hair is curly, you iron it straight; if it's straight, you curl-iron it. If you're short, you want to be a volleyball star; if you're tall, you want to be a Tinker Bell. No one wants whatever color eyes they have. There is no girl in the history of womankind who thought her boobs and butt were the right size. Fat thighs are a common lament. Some girls have singular obsessions. I had a friend who was crazed over *soft elbows*; she worried that everyone had softer elbows than her.

You are still at a mostly fabulous age: you look in the mirror and say, "Oh, I'm sooooo *beauuuuuuuuteeeeful.*" But the older you get, the more I hear those preludes to puberty: "My legs are fat; my lips are too little; I want blond hair . . ." Those words are like fingernails on a blackboard to me.

I promise someday you will be happy with you. I used to obsess over the belief that my thighs were too big. Then one day I spied a big, sturdy brunette with defensive-back thighs who wore black leggings and a lace camisole under a flowing red Chinese robe. By conventional standards, she was a walking page from one of those "Would you be caught dead wearing this outfit?" tabloid articles. But you could tell by her confidence, by the way she carried herself, that by *her* standards, she was stunning! Breathtaking! Lesson: It's only a figure fault if you let it be. Be yourself.

Tip #3: Fashion is a science. Say wrapping a behemoth butt in Spandex strikes you as more crazy than courageous; there's a whole wide world of other fashion statements you can make. You can work with anything or around anything. Figure out your flattering styles and colors. Patterns, textures, fabrics, accessories can make or break a look.

If comfort and style are in a dead heat, opt for comfort. I've tried my whole life to wear those fabulous fuzzy mohairs. Since I was a kid, I've refused to accept that I'm allergic to wool, but I am. So year after year, I buy, wear, itch, toss. Same with high heels. I love them and keep buying them, and without fail, within an hour of my putting them on, my feet and calves cramp into rigor mortis.

When you're shopping, remember that you get what you pay for. It's better to have a few good frocks than closets full of crud. I'd rather be whipped than go clothes shopping. So I get good clothes; they last longer and look better. You won't get your good clothes graduate shopping degree until you discover and develop your own tastes.

That requires shopping discipline and study. I realize that defeats the point of shopping when you're young.

Don't neglect the therapeutic qualities of shopping. Shopping can be a reward for good behavior; a pick-me-up when you're down (a new purse is better than Prozac); mindless entertainment. Malls are for meandering. Shopping there is a rite of passage. In its purest form, shopping isn't about actually purchasing with a purpose. Purposeful shopping is a drag: Christmas and grocery shopping are pure drudgery. But Tar-jhay can be a treasure hunt. Wandering around Wal-Mart can be a quest. (Or maybe I'm just trying to convince myself that we're having fun, since those are our all-time-favorite field trips.)

Tip #4: Everybody has bad hair days. The time and money you'll spend on your hair will exceed the GNP of Liechtenstein. There are as many hairdo horror stories as bad diets. But let me get to the point. In hair as in blind dates, less is more. Don't fool around too much.

Regular, hard brushing stimulates hair follicles and disseminates natural oils for healthier hair. I'm not just saying this because I'm tired of brushing out rats' nests because you girls only groom the ten strands of hair on top of your heads and not the shaggy underbrush. Okay, yes, I am.

Never hold a hot blow dryer directly on your hair; that

icky smell is your hair burning. Wiggle the dryer around or you will smell like a dead dog.

Obviously, keep your hair clean, but don't wash it every day or it will turn into straw. (I guarantee you will go through this phase, despite the fact that hair washing now is your own personal hell.)

Don't let your girlfriends fool with your hair; chemicals and coloring are really dangerous in inexperienced hands. When I was a beauty school student, my African American classmates turned my waist-length hair into an afro worthy of the *Guinness Book of World Records*. Once Aunt Gracie got a perm and frosting too close together, and her hair turned into a Brillo pad. Using cosmetology contacts, I found her some exotic sheep placenta, guaranteed to correct any hair mishap. It turned her hair green. After trying multiple other miracle cures, she finally just shaved her head and wore a hat for six weeks!

Stay away from any and all heads of hair if you're depressed or have PMS or are under the influence. Once when Maria and I had too much wine, I gave her a brush cut by accident. We were sitting on the floor using the sliding glass patio doors as our mirror, which skewed my perspective. In law school I accidentally gave *myself* a brush cut since I'd *lost all* perspective.

Wait for fads to show some staying power before you try them on yourself. We moved pretty quickly through the Sinéad O'Connor shaved-head and purple-streak grunge trends. On the other hand, the Farrah Fawcett wings have made a comeback! Remember that you'll have to live with any hair faux pas for weeks, if not months, and your do will be a don't in photo albums—or online, in the era of digital cameras—for all time. Think how you laugh your way through my old photos. Do you want your kids doing that to you?

Tip #5: When you apply makeup, use good products in the right color *sparingly*. Yeah, right. That's why I have three drawers full of makeup!

Really, there's only one thing you need to know about beauty: You are, by far, on all the earth, in all of history, *the two most beautiful girls God ever created or ever will*.

Love,
A Fellow Beauty Queen

SEASONED CITIZENS

Dear Generation Z,

We talk a lot about r-e-s-p-e-c-t, for others and for yourself. Showing respect is mandatory and not just because it's good manners. Some folks may not deserve the respect you show, but there's one group of people for whom you must err on the side of respect no matter what: the elderly.

You don't have as much exposure to old folks as Daddy and I did, and these times don't exalt elders as ours did. Or maybe it was our ethnic cultures or family values. When and where I grew up, everyone took care of their parents. I never heard of a nursing home. When Daddy's mama, Miss Nippy, was bedridden and slipping in and out of consciousness, his five sisters took turns caring for her at Aunt Mary Ann's home. Though they each had their own families, they would alternate nights with Miss Nippy—

feeding her, combing her hair, holding her hand, telling her jokes. Though she responded to very little, they never altered their vigil. She died in that room with her family at her bedside.

You were just toddlers and this home care scared you; it would have seemed absolutely natural to you if you had had a chance to know Miss Nippy better. She was a woman of grand gestures, endless individual kindnesses. She was the "belle of the ball" in ways unique to charming, charmed southern ladies. She was a gourmet cook, a legendary card master, a magnetic raconteur. She was pure grace and class without any pretensions. I'm not saying this as her daughter-in-law (although she was especially grateful for me, since I delivered her highest ambition for her oldest son: marriage and children); you can ask anyone in a one-hundred-mile radius of Carville, Louisiana, about Miss Nippy and be answered with universal, reverential delight.

That was your dad's mother, your grandmother. What a hoot. And what an extraordinary example of an esteemed elder.

My dad's mother, my special Gram, carried herself with the same pride and dignity but in thoroughly different circumstances. As an Eastern European immigrant, she brought with her history and stories and culture that were far from our understanding. What we did see and admire was her determination and grit in her adopted country. An uneducated, "foreign" woman in inhospitable times, she managed to become a hospital dietitian, raise three kids (one with polio) during the Depression, care for *her* mother, and provide the kind of home demanded by men of that background and generation. Her house was always spotless, and even though she had little money, her table was always overloaded with ethnic delicacies.

I couldn't get enough of Gram, and since I was the first grandbaby of her oldest son, I spent much of my childhood basking in her attention. She loved without limit. I never heard her raise her voice, complain, swear, or gossip. She always got me the hippest clothes and jewelry, which was odd, since she was "old country." Although she had married at seventeen and could never even contemplate the opportunities I had in store, we were total soul mates.

I wish you could have known these very different and equally extraordinary older women, not just to have those special people in your life, but to have a natural connection to a generation far removed from yours. Knowing them would have taught you that keen respect that those who've lived long and large deserve; their presence would have transported you through personal histories to the times that made you who you are and this country what it is.

Nothing beats listening to old-timers stories, to learn perspective and wisdom won only through time and experience, to appreciate values tested and found true by time, and to catch their still twinkling tales.

I suspect Daddy and I will feel like old-timers by the time you get around to appreciating our tales (if ever!), but I hope you will seek out, befriend, listen to, and learn from other seniors as well. They will color and enrich your life tapestries in ways that books or even your own experiences can't.

So go adopt a "seasoned citizen."

And don't even think of volunteering your parents to be your friends' adoptees!

XOXO,
Mom

James and myself with Matty and Emma, 2003.

OUR HEARTS BELONG
TO DADDY

Dear Daddy's Girls,

I'm a voracious reader of biographies, particularly the profiles of America's most illustrious politicians and history makers. These are the people who inspire me with their courage, ingenuity, and stick-to-itiveness. Which American hero do I admire more than anyone else in the world? No contest: my dad.

Dad's parents met on the boat from Croatia. They came here with nothing, and my father grew up in a house where nothing but Croatian was ever spoken at home. He held a bunch of blue-collar jobs, served in the air force in the Korean War, then came home and worked the swing shift at the steel mill while he got his bachelor's degree in mechanical engineering on the GI Bill. He and Ma had us three kids. And he did it all without ever missing a day of work. He taught himself how to sail and ski—truly odd pursuits in our solidly blue-collar neighborhood—because these were sports where he could challenge himself, measure himself against his last performance or fastest time, and constantly seek to better himself. In his forties, having risen through the management ranks at U. S. Steel, he earned his MBA at Purdue and taught himself the commodities market—again, an unusual field, when everyone around us earned an hourly wage. Dad passed that work ethic on to me and my siblings.

While Ma mostly shared her life lessons over our many sessions of kitchen-table wisdom, Dad took every opportunity to explain the practicalities of the world to me. I remember his taking me to the beach to show me how, when the waves retreated, flocks of tiny birds would come skittering out of the sky and eat the sea creatures the tide had left behind. "That's survival of the fittest," he told me. "Every piece of nature shows how every single creature on earth has adapted to stay alive." Dad, the ultimate Darwinist, used this as an example to tell us, "You're in charge of yourself; don't expect anyone else to take care of you." Then he'd show me how the stars fit into constellations, how collectively they were so much more beautiful than individual points of light. That was his introduction to the importance of taking care of your family, your community, your country; to the truth that together we're so much more important than our individual selves.

Dad would never have called himself a feminist, but he

was totally gender-blind and never made a distinction between us girls and our brother. He simply expected all of us to do our best. Anything worth doing was worth doing with absolute commitment. He convinced me that math is a wonderful thing. Being Croatian, we all had to play accordion (this has made me the woman I am today). He taught himself guitar. Then he put the whole family into a band, with Ma on bass, Renie on banjo, Steve on drums, and me where I could do the least damage.

Without a doubt, I worship my father. My dad gave me my passion for politics, economics, history. He lived by the old-country values—friendship, honor, duty to family and community—that his people transplanted to America and he practiced daily in our home. He was and is always an attentive and thoughtful dad. When I was little, to instill confidence, he'd take me to the mall, where we'd sit on a bench and watch the people go by. "You're prettier than that one," he'd tell me. "You're smarter than this one. You just need to have confidence. Look at these people; ninety-nine percent of them are stupider and uglier than you." When I got my first adult job he told me, "Don't be intimidated by your coworkers. They don't have anything you don't have; they just have more experience." He was absolutely convinced that I had what it took to do what I wanted to do. In confusing situations, I can hear his voice in my head: "There's no other option but honesty." "There's no such thing as quitting."

Moms are the oxygen children breathe; dads are the water they swim in. Whatever confidence I have today comes from two loving, complementary sources: Ma's unconditional love and my dad's relentlessly practical illustrations of his unflagging belief in me.

The same doting double-teaming is at work in our family. Just as my dad gave me things that Ma couldn't, Daddy fills roles for you two that I'm not suited for. Where else will you learn the art of full-body enthusiasm—this from a man whose longest span of concentration is that required to make his special French fries or French toast—for the silliest enterprise, whether it's LSU football (not that I think for one nanosecond that southerners' extreme football fanaticism is silly) or beating me at gin rummy? Who better to teach you how to appreciate everything to the max? (Daddy's always declaring, "You're the best wife I've ever had!" "This is the best gumbo ever!")

Daddy is teaching you how to be light. He'll tell the same dumb joke over and over and over, just to make you groan with laughter. He lets you make him the butt of all your family jokes. He has an incredible joie de vivre. He's a relentless teaser. Right now his running joke is that you're going to go to finishing school—learn how to set a proper table, be immaculately groomed for a four-o'clock white-glove tea. "I think, girls, we should gather around and have a family discussion and talk pleasantly about what did we do at school." He's blind to the disparity between the sort of angelic girls who sit with legs daintily crossed at the Plaza and you real-life Eloises tumbling around on the carpet. He stomps around pretending to be the disciplinarian while we all just roll our eyes. "You're not going to think *that's* so funny when you're in Mrs. J. Primpington III's finishing school!"

I can compliment your looks until the cows come home, but no one makes you feel like princesses like your daddy does—like you're each the most beautiful, elegant, desirable God's gift that ever walked the earth. When you have your hair combed special and get all dressed up, you blow me off to show off for "Daddy, Daddy!" He's always asking everyone, and I mean everyone—total strangers who stop us on the street—"Have you ever seen girls more smart or beautiful than mine?" (Elbowing him in the ribs, hissing, "Shut *up!*" has no effect.) It's Daddy's gift that he can make you and all your girlfriends feel beautiful and worthy. It answers some call that I can't answer when you can be beautiful for your father—not girly beautiful, but special, unique. I'm not talking just about looks here. It's that same sense my dad imbued me with: "Anyone would be lucky to be walking behind you, cleaning up your droppings." If you can hold on to that feeling your whole life, you'll be lucky indeed.

He takes his role as steward of your education a little too much to heart. Since he used to be a science teacher, he can get really pedantic. When Matty asked him, "How did World War I get started?" Daddy responded, "As Bismarck said, 'Some damn fool thing in the Balkans.'" That really cleared it up for an eight-year-old!

I can't quite figure out how Daddy got his romantic vision of family, a fantasy family so stuck in the fifties, with himself the strutting patriarch and everyone driving around in the big-finned Chevrolet. I think he's still stunned to find himself an accidental tourist in the marriage and family business. He never thought he'd have a wife, let alone kids; he'd led a nomadic life until he got married at forty-nine. Now he's just fascinated by his daughters in the way southern men are. He never wants to talk about politics and current events when he calls from the road or at the end of the day; for him it's the Matty & Emma Special all the time.

Of course, the flip side of all that adoration is that he worries to death over every little thing. I get the third degree after every school event he had to miss: "What did the teacher say?" "How did Emma feel about herself?" When Matty had to get glasses—hardly a sign of an exotic disease—he scoured the country for the eye man of the century. The poor guy's already grilling me about what's gonna happen with pierced ears, short skirts, mean girls, fast boys . . . He comes up with a new future worry every day!

My dad and your daddy differ in a thousand ways, but they share a special talent: the ability to see not past your faults, but through them, to the good stuff waiting to get out. Matty, remember when you were upset because you thought your handwriting was so unlovely? Daddy didn't pooh-pooh your concerns, but he showed you how to look beyond them, showed you that having a million ideas spilling out so fast that you don't have time to write them down with perfect penmanship can also be a sign of creativity and energy.

The three of us have a lot of fun ganging up on Daddy, making fun of him. I'll be the first to admit that I usually lead the charge, but in fact I'm always moved and tremendously proud of how seriously Daddy takes his role. I've spent my whole life trying to live up to my dad's high opinion of me—a worthy goal I'll never stop striving for. I hope you'll have the same goal. I promise you that you'll always find the challenge worthwhile, and that your Daddy will always deserve it.

XOXO,
Mom

SISTER, SISTER

Dear Sisters,

Matty, the other day you drew yourself up to your full eight-year-old height and informed me indignantly, "Ever since Emma's in my school, she's invading my personal space!" Emma complained, "Matty's always the best, she's always the first!" I just looked at you both and told you what I've told you a hundred times before, what I'll tell you ten thousand times more: "You are *so lucky* to have a sister!"

I should know. I was two years and three months old when my sister, Irene Marie, was born. Up until that point, I'd been pretty happy to have Patti Playpal, whose main draw was that she was big enough for me to smack around. From that day forward, Renie has been my most beloved best friend. We were, and still are, constant playmates; I would cut her hair (I once cut it to make her look like Cher, circa 1966), dress her up, experiment with makeup on her; I was her personal consultant on boys and I even took her to her first rock concert.

Even as a toddler Renie was steadfast. She taught me everything I needed to know about holding your ground. She wouldn't budge if she didn't get what she wanted. She would hold her breath until she literally turned blue. Someone would have to take her to Gram's sink, turn her upside down, and put her head under the cold water to get her breathing again. I was speechless with admiration.

We've always been opposites. I'm always flighty; Renie's always grounded. I was always racing ahead to the next stage, desperate to be an adult. Renie was very secure, happy to be the age she was. I ran pell-mell toward an uncertain future; Renie methodically planned a life with all the milestones: education, marriage, kids. Even though I'm older, she's the more mature, smarter one. Between the two of us, we're one complete person. We figured out pretty early on how to merge as that one person. Whoever was good at the task at hand would take the lead, and we would just hand off to each other from grade school on.

Renie tells me I pulled away a little bit when I got out of junior high; suddenly I was acting grown up and Renie was still a kid. She was still playing with toys, I was getting calls from boys. Once we both hit high school, we were back on the same wavelength. We did a lot together— pom-pom girls, student council, football games, concerts. We looked out for each other and hardly ever fought, except over clothes. She'd unscrew the padlock on my closet door and heist my best outfits. (I inherited Ma's eye for fashion while Renie swore she was color-blind.) Then she'd avoid me in the hallways at school so I wouldn't catch her in my ensembles! Of course, I would anyway and we'd get into screaming fights. If Ma walked in on one of our fights, she would just say, "You two don't know how lucky you are to have a sister." Ma had two brothers, and she always longed for the closeness that only a sister can provide.

When Renie was a high school freshman, I was a junior. I seriously hated high school; Renie loved it. She orchestrated a flanking maneuver to get all the freshmen to vote me in as Homecoming Queen; I was nowhere near the prettiest, nicest, or most popular, but thanks to Renie's strategizing, the other, more qualified girls split the vote amongst themselves and she got me elected!

Renie continued to be the power behind the throne when we both went off to the same college. The "pretty one" and the "smart one" became the "party one" and the "smart one." Renie was a brilliant student who worked hard and got straight As—plus one B for swimming, which I made her take with me. Then I dropped out of the (8 AM!) class; she stuck it out, and that single B marred her perfect record. All throughout college, I was running around getting into everything. I had at least four majors and more boyfriends during any given semester. Renie just kept her head down and ticked off her goals one by one, and that meant only one boyfriend at a time. It took me seven years to graduate from college; of course, Renie finished early.

In our twenties we took wildly divergent paths but always stayed close. Renie got her degree in special education, moved back home with Ma and Dad, got engaged, got married, and then had Patrick, Erin, and Kevin. She stayed home with them, only returning to teaching when they were in school. I zigzagged around the country on the campaign trail, never thinking about settling down, since being aunt to Renie's kids was just like having my own, maybe better, since I had no diaper duty or anything that remotely smacked of responsibility, only fun!

Renie always plans for every contingency. A simple trip to the zoo became the Raid on Entebbe: Renie, making us synchronize our watches, would say something like, "If Patrick falls into the lion's den, and the lion gets a burst of testosterone, and the monkeys jump in, and the giraffe falls over, then we'll . . ." Meanwhile, the one time she put me in charge at the National Air and Space Museum, it took me less than three minutes to lose Patrick (then only four years old), my own godson! Renie flew into action and got the whole place in lockdown in no time flat. I stood paralyzed for the next few terrifying minutes, until she found him by sheer mother instinct—hidden in a rocket!

When I became a mom, Renie was the only one who could assuage my back-to-back panic attacks. When we were younger and Renie had questions about growing up, she came to me; now I go to her when I have a mommy question, and you two are fortunate for her always-great advice. I'm the authority on neurotic behavior and impractical thinking; Renie has the market cornered on maternal instinct.

To this day your aunt Renie is my best friend. She's the first one there in the toughest places—from Poppy's cancer to Uncle Steve's spinal cord injury—and the best one in the soft places: she never forgets a birthday, anniversary, or any special event. She calms everyone down in calamities and can organize us all in our worst ADHD outrages. She's relentlessly open and fair-minded. She's the Zen of zone. She's a crazed mother tiger if you're in trouble. She can do anything, including make me think I can do anything. Although we don't share a political philosophy, she's my one-woman focus group, the canary in the coal mine who keeps me grounded. If I'm on the phone with her and Daddy walks in, I just say, "I'm on with Renie," and he knows to blow out. Could be three minutes, could be three hours, but it will always be totally engrossing. Daddy always says to me, accusingly, "You *never* don't take Renie's side, no matter what the situation." I tell him, "That's because Renie is never wrong!" Renie and I don't even have to talk to know what the other's thinking. If I pick up the phone and it's her, I can tell from the first breath: "Okay, what's wrong?" We can read each other's minds, so it's lucky we have no secrets.

My sister is flawless. She's a saint. I love her with a love like only one other—the limitless way I love you two—with every single fiber of my being.

I always knew I wanted Matty to have a sister, because of what I've had with Renie, although it took a bit of doing at age forty-five. I kept persevering through many disappointments; the whole time Renie was thinking, "This is all my fault"—for being such a great sister!—and I was thinking, "Oh God, what if it's a boy?" Finally, after two years and nine months—almost exactly the same spacing as between Renie and me!—we had Emma. It's almost scary, but each of you is a combination of the both of us.

A lot of women with sisters have told me they can't imagine the relationship Renie and I enjoy. Many sisters we know constantly bicker or have periodic major blowouts. New friends think we're either the biggest dweebs or in denial. We may very well be the dweeb sisters, but our devotion is real and relentless. It transcends that more familiar familial bond of obligation. We are always there for each other, not because it's the right thing to do; it's the *only* way we know.

Although we never took this blessing for granted, we are more mindful of its beauty as we watch you two developing the same connection. Sure you have your fights, but you revere each other. God forbid anyone else—including Daddy or me—criticizes either of you. My all-time favorite exchange is when one of you comes whining to me about some dirty deed done by the other. Then I yell at the dirty-deed doer. Then you yell at me for taking *your* side!

You write about each other, brag about each other, bring each other to show and tell. Your teachers all comment on your special closeness.

I can't tell you how completely happy this makes me but, even more, how much joy and fulfillment it will mean to you throughout your lives.

So, girls, appreciate what you've got. Of course, in our household we've got the female superiority thing going: everything you see is what Daddy calls "gynodynamics." The women all around you—Renie and I, plus all of Daddy's five sisters and my girlfriends, your other "aunts"—are tough and strong and run stuff; we definitely rule the world (or at least *think* we do!). You will also have your own gynodynamic dynasties, but your most very special universe of just you two will always be your precious place to take refuge in, rely on, relax into.

In sister solidarity,
Mom

P.S. You'd still better lock your closets!

SENIOR MOMENT

Dear Young Ones,

In my last hair makeover, I went short-short. Of course, I thought it was chic and sophisticated—and, most important, convenient: just blow and go. But Daddy totally missed the point. He thought I went punk rock: Joan Jett meets Rod Stewart. I was stunned for two reasons. First, Daddy never notices even the most dramatic changes in my hairdos. In my distractible days of Matty's toddlerhood, I screwed up my hair so badly I had to go in for a radical do-over. I went from a long, butchered mane in every hue of orange to a short, dark bob. I barely recognized myself, yet Daddy didn't give me a second glance! Second, he insisted I cut my hair to look younger as an act of rebellion against turning fifty. He wouldn't believe me when I told him I wasn't trying to look *any other* age, only trying to look like me at *this* age.

The new haircut changed the balance and color of my highlights. I had been looking like a zebra that had rolled around in elephant dung; it was time to go back to the salon and back to my natural color—mousy brown. I was still in the animal kingdom, just closer to home.

This time my friend Steven noticed and said, "It's great; it makes you look so much younger!" To which I screamed, "I don't *want* to look younger! I just want to look like me! *This is what I look like!*" I think we can agree that Mommy overreacted just a teeny bit.

Later, pondering my outburst at that sweet man's innocent compliment and my vehement objection to Daddy's theory of haircut as pathetic time machine, I figured I was having some subliminal negative reaction to turning fifty. Everyone, *everyone* asked me (in a sorrowful tone) how did I feel turning the big five-oh? Other than my superstitious need to get past the age my mom was when she died, I felt nothing. Not bad, not good, not reflective—nothing.

Clearly, turning fifty meant something—something not good—to the rest of the world. Try as I might, though, I just couldn't get depressed about it (and I am a master at depression on command). In fact, the more I thought about it, the more I realized that if I felt anything, it was pretty close to exhilaration. Liberation. Excitement. Anticipation. I think I overreacted to Steven and Daddy because I was confused and frustrated that they would presume that I wanted to look younger because I didn't like looking my age.

Well, who could blame them? Our country is obsessed with staying young. Perfectly well adjusted, accomplished grown women regularly make fools of themselves in Britney Spears getups. Worse, some men change not only their wardrobe but their wives.

Something may be wrong with me, but—at least for now—I so do not care about aging. I care a lot about staying healthy, which requires more attention as you age. The good news is that what it takes to stay healthy also makes you feel good. When you feel good, you look good, so you get lots of positive reinforcement. I've made the necessary accommodations—more sleep, more exercise, less wine, no ciggies—but they're no big deal. Except for the massive mood swings and memory loss, even menopause is just another adaptation. (Other than that, Mrs. Lincoln, how was the play?)

So it's always a shock when you guys tell me how old I am. Your favorite way to express this is "Mom, get out of the *eighties!*" or "Were there telephones when you were little?" or "What was Abraham Lincoln like?" You tell your friends, "My mom was alive when there were *hippies!*" Nevertheless, not only do I not feel old, I've never felt better.

I think I take getting older in stride because my parents set such a solid example for me. They lived by my mom's adage, "You're only as old as you feel." They always had youthful hobbies, habits, and mind-sets. My mom always had a contemporary wardrobe; I used to borrow her hot pants (a sartorial sin; who invents these ridiculous fashions?). She liked (most of) our music, got our jokes, never objected to my black-light bedroom décor, took painting and pottery classes, and got a player piano so she could belt out tunes (in the single worst voice known to mankind—worse than Daddy's, even). She loved hanging out with us and was so popular that my old boyfriends kept visiting her long after our relationships faded. She ran a beauty school; her students were all right out of high school (or younger, some were high school dropouts) and they all related to her, loved her. At Aunt Renie's college graduation party, she fit right in with the rowdy, loud, overindulging revelers.

Of course, seeing the world through your eyes helps keep me feeling young too. You bring home today's vocabulary, like "rad" or "bad," which both mean "good." You have modern comebacks, so when I say, "Two wrongs don't make a right," you say, "But two rights make a left." We like the same music and movies. And the fact that your daddy has a serious case of arrested development slows down the hourglass for both of us. Your aunt Renie and my girlfriends are also there to put senior moments in perspective. Renie is always losing her car keys. Yesterday I lost my *car*, but I figured that was in the same family of spacyness.

I never got into age phobia. As far back as I can remember, I always wanted to be an adult—independent, self-assured, and in charge. Beyond book learning, I wanted wisdom, judgment, and good sense, traits I believed came only through aging. Now that I've actually become an adult, I realize that none of those aspirations have anything to do with age. Becoming your own person takes more effort than just cruising through the years.

I know that, at ages eight and six, you want to be older and try to act older. But when you *are* older, you'll yearn for youth. Try to live in the moment, because the reality is that each age and phase brings unique joys and breakthroughs. You make new discoveries and gain wisdom, judgment, and patience, which enhance each age and deepen over time.

Your teens and twenties are a treasure trove of new knowledge; facts and ideas hit you with hurricane force. Stay open to them and don't feel pressed to put them in order. That will come with time. Use those years to expose yourself to the world's wonders, to expand your thinking and reasoning. Make sure school isn't your only place of learning.

By your thirties, some unseen force nudges you to maturity. Personally and professionally you start wanting to put your life in some semblance of order. This may not necessarily mean settling down with one person or settling into a career. But most people begin pulling together their priorities. Guided by their individual goals, they set out on a course, order their actions into a direction. The combination of skills acquired in your twenties and the growing self-knowledge and direction of your thirties leads to more interesting and fulfilling life decisions at work and home.

For all the negatives attached to the forties, it can be a time of peak performance. Rush Limbaugh once told me you don't make money until your forties, which is generally true, as that's the time you advance in your chosen field and are commensurately compensated. Money means security and comfort, but best of all, it gives you options.

In your fifties, you have the attitude to pursue those options. You go for things because they're fun, not just because they make money. Your friendships are deeper, your marriage has more meaning, your concern for the opinions or validation of others diminishes. You gain perspective and purpose. Can you tell I love my fifties? I've loved every age, once I started working and making my own passage.

You've got some amazing role models for the years ahead. My dad is seventy-five, works full-time, and goes dancing, dining, and golfing with his fun wife, Grama Barb, despite his cancer diagnosis. I know plenty of people younger than they are who never got over getting over thirty; they act like each day is designed to just get through. Not Poppy and Grama Barb.

No one in Daddy's family ever ages. They live and love life every day and then they die. Seriously, at every funeral, all the siblings say the same thing in their own way: what a great life the departed led and how grateful they are to have had a part in it. I pray you inherit their belief in the beauty of each and every day, their gratitude for God's gift of life. Daddy's mama's joie de vivre was cranked up high right up till her Alzheimer's fade in her eighties.

Daddy and I get such a thrill watching you grow. Between your genes and your upbringing, I feel confident you'll like every age too.

I remember exactly how I felt about older people when I was your age, so I'm not expecting you to appreciate what I'm telling you right now. Just promise me you'll reread this letter every few years. Take that time to revel in your life's journey. Embrace aging. Think of it as advancing. Enjoy each stage. Mark milestones and make memories. Live large.

Of course you'll have your pitfalls, push-backs, even disasters at every age. There were plenty of times I was depressed in my teens, distraught in my twenties, disorganized in my thirties, disillusioned in my forties. I still have days of dismay. My mom had several useful bromides she applied to these inevitable upsets at any age: 1) Learn from your mistakes, 2) Keep everything in perspective, 3) Time heals all wounds, and no matter how painful, 4) This too shall pass.

I'd like to give you more fresh-faced guidance, but I've yet to find any that works better than Ma's has for me.

I promise you that when I'm not around to protect you, there is nothing you can't handle. For every bad deal, there'll be countless great adventures. *Seize* them.

And when you take off on those grand adventures, think about taking your old geezer mom along.

Love,
The Old Gray Mare

TAKING THE HIGH ROAD

Dear Future Trailblazers,

My mom was always getting me out of jams and often blamed herself for my bad decisions. In an effort to absolve her of responsibility for my actions I gave her, with love and gratitude, a plaque that read, THE ONLY LEGACY ONE SHOULD LEAVE THEIR CHILDREN IS ROOTS AND WINGS. When my mom passed, my dad gave the plaque back to me. It sits on my makeup table, where I read it every day, to no effect.

Now that I lie awake at night blaming myself for your tiniest issues, I understand this maternal neurosis. It was neither her job nor in her capacity to make me happy any more than I can command sunshine for you every day. Not that that stops me from trying or going crazy when I fail. You will be the same way with your kids. (You are already overprotective of each other).

As much as my mom would have loved to have been able to make my decisions, as much as I might love to make your decisions forever, you have to make your own choices and live with the consequences of those choices. Even when events seem beyond your control—stuff just happens to you or others treat you a certain way—you still always have the ultimate control because *you choose* how to react to the unexpected event or treatment.

Some days you may feel like Yogi Berra: "When you come to a fork in the road, take it." Oh, how we all wish we could! Girls, when you come to one of those confusing crossroads, you have to choose. It probably will never seem this simple, but as a general rule, you'll have two choices: you can either take the high road or the low road.

The low road is easier and more instantly gratifying but usually leads to uneasiness at a minimum, and over time, cynicism. The high road takes patience, resilience, humility, vision, compassion. Sometimes it's lonely, but you're shooting for a place you want to be in the end—confident of and comfortable with your choices. Unless you're a hermit, you'll find life with other human beings full of unexpected jolts, from petty grievances to ugly indignities: witchy girlfriends, bad boyfriends, mean teachers, unfair bosses, blithering idiocies, and stunning corruptions.

Your first instinct will be to respond in kind. My mother was too dignified to "sink to their level" when she had to deal with dopes. Her stoic response to inequitable behavior was "What goes around comes around."

As we used to say at your age, there's good karma and bad karma. Acting with dignity and grace begets good karma; responding with revenge and anger are the stuff of bad karma. The point is, *you* make the karma.

You may laugh at this hippie lingo, but the truth is you create your own reality. That reality isn't what happens to you but how you respond. That's the reality you have to live in. So, gals, remember your roots, be confident in your flight, and on your life journey when you come to a fork, hit the high road.

XOXO,
Mom

BABY, REMEMBER YOUR NAME

Dear Girls,

You two both keep saying, "I want to be famous. I'm going to be famous." Matty just asked Emma, "Would you rather have fame and fortune or me as your big sister?" Emma, without hesitation, replied, "Fame." This is a topic that never crossed my mind when I was your age. I do remember dreaming that when I was a grown up I would be accomplished at something, anything.

As I got older, it dawned on me that it was possible to accomplish something *and get paid for it.* Then, as I really matured, I wanted to be paid AND *respected* for my accomplishments. While this might sound evolved, let me point out that obsessive hungering for respect from others is in fact truly immature, although our entire culture seems to have the same craving. Real grown-ups act out of a sense of self-respect and personal integrity. Alas, ladies, the older you get, the more you'll find out how few real adults there are! (Ironically, personal growth gurus have become a thriving cottage industry, each expert seeking the external acknowledgment he or she counsels against.)

When I was your age, fame was a foreign concept. We were taught that the whole point of adult work was to provide for yourself and family. The aim was to give your kids a start and have something left over to avoid being a burden in retirement. The values were simple and universal: A penny saved is a penny earned. A good day's pay for a hard day's work. The harder your work, the greater your return. In those days your personal worth was measured by your productivity, and your productivity determined your net worth. We called it blood money, sweat equity. Growing up, I never knew anyone who wasn't paid by the hour. No one in the family or neighborhood was paid for "consulting" or "creative input." No one made money off investments. Stocks were bequeathed to widows so they could live on the meager dividends. I was an hourly wage earner for every job I held from age eleven until well into my twenties.

Fame simply wasn't a kitchen-table topic of conversation at our house or *any* house in our neighborhood. My brother, sister, and I and almost every kid we knew were the first generation to go to college, but we all went to get a better job. No one wanted to be famous; that was the exclusive province of movie stars. In those days, if you wanted to be a movie star, it was often because they were living examples (or at least their on-screen characters were) of the most highly regarded values and virtues—Scarlett O'Hara, the Lone Ranger, Lancelot. (No, I am *not* that old; I just was more impressed with older movies.) Stars weren't idols because they were famous; they were famous because they portrayed something or someone worth idolizing.

But you girls just want to be famous. Famous for what? Fame means being renowned. You have to be renowned for doing or accomplishing something, not just for being.

Right now, your concept of fame is being on TV, mostly because Daddy and I are on TV. You don't understand that we're on TV *doing something*. Specifically, we're advocates or defenders for our respective points of view and the people who represent them.

To you, those talk (shout) shows are BOOORRRING. There's no story, no learning, no laughs (though we certainly have critics who do find us laughable—mostly people who want to be on TV!). What you *do* get is your classmates' saying, "I saw your mom/dad on TV!" Just being on TV impresses them. Even better is when they see you on Tim Russert, where you don't do anything except be incredibly cute, which likely reinforces your notion that that's all you need to be famous! Daddy has a theory: once you're famous, you can't do anything else but be famous. It's true, in his case, that just being "James Carville" is a purpose in and of itself. But Daddy was James Carville before he was "James Carville." (Sometimes even he can momentarily forget that, but we level him pretty fast!)

Actually, today people can be famous for doing nothing. So-called reality TV is going through a really lame phase of granting fame to people for just showing up and fulfilling some lunatic idea of good entertainment, like eating cow eyeballs or making out with some dork who is picking out a wife through that most intimate of venues, national prime-time television. Or you can become famous by really doing nothing; just put a minicam in your house and live!

It's also true in this age that you can be famous for being infamous, like too many truly nasty recording "artists." These people actually, specifically, doggedly strive for infamy! Can you believe being bad is their basis for fame? (Even more astounding, their awfulness is revered and promoted as "art" or "free speech" or "the creative process." They are revered mostly by uncreative groupthinkers who believe that only *their* speech and art are defensible.)

Seeking fame is fine so long as you understand that you have to work hard and well at something worthwhile. "Worthwhile" doesn't have to mean monumental, like you're Mother Teresa or Sally Ride or Mia Hamm. Whatever you do has to be worthwhile *to you*. And it can be, actually, *should* be fun.

To me the most worthwhile and fun job of all time is campaigning, but after the Republicans lost in 1992, I was personally radioactive. No one would hire me in politics. Just to pay the bills, I agreed to cohost an experimental show on a cable network whose only requirement was that the hosts be women. Just because we were females and by definition gave the nightly all-male lineup balance, they started out basically letting us do our thing. The show was named *Equal Time*, but I called it *Wayne's World on Estrogen*.

Much to my amazement and grand amusement, the show gained a measure of cultish fame. I did work really hard to learn the subject matter and our guests' views on it, but very often the show collapsed into chaotic hilarity *live*.

One time Daddy flew all the way back from Europe to shock me silly on my fortieth birthday as a surprise on the show. The hilarious cohost, Jane Wallace, and I announced my engagement by singing into a hairbrush, "Going to the chapel and we're gonna get married" while the guest, John King, a serious journalist (and incredibly great sport) rolled his eyes. On subsequent episodes, sports guru journalist Tony Kornheiser became the master hairbrush crooner, despite having little reason to have any hairbrushes. At a time when TV bosses usually want to take women off the air, I stayed on the air through my entire Matty pregnancy, getting fatter and bigger. I was joined by a generous guest cohost, the late Bob Squire, who threw a red velvet cloth over a giant watermelon sitting on his lap so we could be TV Twinkies.

Almost everyone we invited accepted and joined the fun, which might include my profusely and unknowingly lactating on air the first show back after pregnancy leave or screaming (I mean *screeching!*) at Jane for making fun of Dan Quayle.

Shockingly, the reviews were great. Our ratings were solid (for cable) and our fans were intense. One reviewer called the show "loopy," so I dubbed its cult followers "loopsters." As you know, because you've been there, ten years later people still come up to me and proclaim, "I'm a loopster!"

The more popular the show got, the less fun it was. The bosses started butting in big time, dictating guests and topics. The fun stopped altogether when the shortsighted management fired my producer because I refused to do any O. J. Simpson shows, declaring *Equal Time* to be an "O. J.-free talk show zone." I fumed and fretted, fulfilled my contract, then quit. No one could believe I would give up a TV show! An opportunity for fame! (The same thing happened years later when I left *Crossfire* to go to the White

House.) It still astounds me how many people would kill their grandma for a TV show. I wasn't looking for fame. I needed a paying job and preferred one that was fun.

I wasn't seeking it and I wasn't afraid to lose it, but TV taught me a lot about fame. Hilary Duff makes fame look like endless fun, but it has some definite down sides. We're hardly household names, yet total strangers treat us like their next-door neighbors. Uninteresting people feel absolutely free to come up to me at any time, in any circumstance, and tell me that I'm an idiot or that my husband's a moron. Or they want me to tell George Bush x, Dick Cheney y. When you're famous, you get guilted into doing events for causes you couldn't care less about. People make stuff up about you to suck up to gossip columnists. You can't yell at stupid people in public places because it will get into the gossip columns. (Daddy once made a column for "talking loudly" during a movie. Daddy never doesn't "talk loudly"!)

We're such small fry, our lost anonymity is more annoying than intrusive. You hate when strangers approach us in airports or restaurants. You demand that we say, "Sorry, I'm with my family." If our occasional interruptions bother you, real fame would blister you. Big-time famous people can't ever walk down a street or eat out or go to the movies or the mall without being accosted. I was truly horrified and mortified at the way Steven Soderbergh and George Clooney were harangued when they were in Washington filming *K Street* for HBO. They were unfailingly gracious, polite, and accommodating to the gushing hordes— signed all autographs, engaged in mindless chatter. Best of all, they stayed their normal selves. As much as I respected their talents, I really admired how they were able to stay centered and balanced.

They gave me great insight into what I really want you to understand about fame. All the famous people you know have stayed true to themselves, but that's not universally the case among the famed. They say power corrupts, but I work in the world of power, and however it may corrupt is nothing compared to how fame corrupts. I've watched at close range as fame converts and corrodes good folks into true jackasses. Many people get blinded and burned by the spotlight. In politics we call it the disease of "reading your own press." Literature is replete with tales of hubris. I never liked those tragedies and like them even less in real life.

Becoming a jerk is one thing. Scarier, and obviously more tragic, is how the pressure of fame—either dealing with it or trying to keep it—can lead to self-destructive behavior, such as alcohol or drugs or illicit sex. Whatever the escape, the upshot is pain and peril—professional and personal. Then follows the inevitable public fall from grace. The press loves to chronicle the failure and self-destruction of the famous. Public humiliation sells.

Obviously, fame can be glorious. Validation for one's

work is fulfilling. It's great to be able to use fame to draw attention to your cherished causes or candidates. You meet interesting people and are offered more diverse opportunities. I'm not telling you *not* to seek fame. I'm trying to make clear that there's more to fame than Hilary Duff's Roman vacation.

So if you really want to be famous, do what you want to do and be your best at it. Don't pursue a career just because it might make you famous. (I guess there's a possibility some people want to eat cow eyeballs and are good at it.)

If you're doing what you love, you're more likely to be great at it and work harder on it. Digging into something you feel passionate about will give you the personal security to withstand the critics and carpers. If your hard work gains you fame, then use it for good. Channel your success; don't let it channel you. And while you're striving, you might paste this quote from Theodore Roosevelt, from a speech he gave at the Sorbonne in 1910, into your personal journals:

It is not the critic who counts: not the man who points out how the strong man stumbles or where the doer of deeds could have done better. The credit belongs to the man who is actually in the arena, whose face is marred by dust and sweat and blood, who strives valiantly, who errs and comes up short again and again, because there is no effort without error or shortcoming, but who knows the great enthusiasms, the great devotions, who spends himself for a worthy cause; who, at the best, knows, in the end, the triumph of high achievement, and who, at the worst, if he fails, at least he fails while daring greatly, so that his place shall never be with those cold and timid souls who knew neither victory nor defeat.

XOXO,
Mom

James and myself, 1993.

MARRIAGE:
ON THE ROAD TO
HAPPILY EVER AFTER

Dear Princesses,

A favorite game of yours to play and mine to eavesdrop on is "We're getting married." You two can play this game without boredom or distraction for hours. You marry each other, alternating who gets to be the bride; conduct multiple Barbie marriages; pair off all your stuffed animals; or simply conduct ceremonies sans any props.

Whatever or whoever the mates, the process is the same: I love you; let's get married; let's get ready for the wedding; here comes the bride. That broad outline is brimming over with minute details of the courting, proposal, wedding plans, walk down the aisle, etc. Curiously, your marriage game ends at the altar; the whole shebang is a big buildup to . . . what? Where's the "happily ever after," the "for better or for worse," the "for richer or poorer"? Sometimes you'll jump to "babies," but I've also seen you play this game without the foreplay of marriage, so it's not clear if you've quite made the connection between the two. (That's another topic we'll surely cover.)

Your fantasy games are fascinating. I don't ever remember playing marriage as a little girl. I had no girlfriends at your age (a geographical anomaly) and really no interest in the subject. The only thing I ever gave much thought to was whether to change my name if I got married. I noodled this concern way before it was PC.

The intensity of your interest in your own pretend marriage is matched by your utter lack of interest in your parents'! You either take it totally for granted or are alternately giggly or grossed out at any manifestations of our marital affections. Matty, you hate when we hold hands and go crazy when we kiss. We like to kiss just to get that "Stop it!" scream. Emma, you always make us kiss and coo. One time Daddy and I were just lying on the bed, enjoying a breezy afternoon at the farm, talking, laughing. For some reason we had the door closed, which, of course, is an automatic invitation to you two to come in. Still, your barging in surprised us and we jumped up like two guilty teens. Matty, you ran out, *"Yuk, yuk, yuk, get up! Get out!"* Emma, you just couldn't stop smiling and prodding, "Kiss, kiss, kiss!" Nature or nurture? Hardwired or recently installed software?

Neither your play marriages nor self-limited view of our marriage is too close to reality. Not that there is only one reality; there are as many definitions of a "good marriage" as there are happily married couples. Each union is unique, and what works for one may be the ruination of another.

My biggest marital issues developed over being constrained by my parents' example. Theirs was a great marriage, but their model doesn't work for us. For example, my parents never fought in front of us. Daddy and I are hammerheads and can't help going at it. We can fight all day over politics, but I had never learned how to fight in a marriage. We figured it out for ourselves, but only after I got over the nagging neurosis that we weren't supposed to be fighting.

It's hard to predict what you will want in your marriages, but you surely will be influenced by what you see growing up. Understand: ours should not be the sole model for your marriage. My advice is to judge your marriage by your standards and needs, no one else's.

Keeping that in mind, here are some marriage tips my mom gave me and a few I picked up myself.

The first rule of marriage in Ma's words was "Look before you leap." I always thought that meant look long and hard at your prospective hubby. But that was only half of the advice. The more important point was to look long and hard at yourself.

Question yourself, by yourself.

Do I want to be married? What is my concept of a good

marriage? What is my mate's concept of a good marriage? Are they compatible? Realistic?

Bounce your conclusions off your girlfriends and mother to see if you're in the reality zone. Then hash it out with your mate. Priests or other spiritual advisers can be helpful at this juncture.

To repeat: you have to have a clear-eyed concept or philosophy of marriage, as does your mate.

I can give personal witness to the importance of this initial effort because I did not make it. I thought because we were older, we were world wise—and marriage wise. It's taken ten years for us to really answer those questions, and I'm not sure that if you all hadn't come along, we would have put in as much reflection as we have. So my perspective is retrospective; it comes from on-the-job training and from observing marriages I admire.

Those simple questions are hard to answer. Being in love with the idea of marriage is not the same as truly wanting to get married. Marriage is not playing house.

Determining your compatibility with your chosen one is especially tricky since men and women don't use the same language. We have the same vocabulary but distinctly different definitions for the same words and concepts. Take the concept "equal partner," for instance, essential in a solid marriage. You mean soul mate, he means income earner. (He also doesn't consider running a home "work.") "Being sensitive to your needs" to you means tap-

ping into your wavelength with no conversation necessary. To him it means making sure his ten-ounce Buds are
perpetually stocked.

Romance for you is going to chick flicks; for him it's
making out at *any* flick!

When you're meeting each other's mothers (for potential insights into your futures), you are laser-focused on
how much respect and reverence he pays his mom. All he
wants to know is how big your mom's bum got as she aged.

So the point is, make sure you define your terms when
you work through addressing those threshold issues.

Once you've determined you really want to be married
and are confident in your compatibility, you will immediately start second-guessing your decision. You will start
having daily, *hourly* bouts of incompatibility. Don't be de-
terred or disheartened. These feelings will recur all
through your marriage. There's always a way to make adjustments for mutual gratification. Right from the beginning, Daddy took the long view on adjusting to each
other. I was convinced our relationship couldn't withstand
the 1992 presidential campaign, when we each served in
high-ranking positions on opposing teams. Careerwise,
we were mortal enemies. Nevertheless, Daddy wrote me a
letter that flat-out asserted we would make it because we
wanted to. He tends to gloss over the details, but this was
his articulation of "Where there's a will, there's a way" (one
of Ma's daily mantras). There's always a way to keep your

marriage compatible. Understand, however, *you* will be in charge of figuring out and executing the details of whatever adjustments your relationship requires.

Here's what I mean. Daddy and I had very disparate ideas of romance when we started to get down to the getdown on the marriage thing. (We have moved closer to each other's romantic concepts over the years—at least understanding, if not always acting on them.)

At the time, we were both more practical than romantic: bottom-line guys, get the job done *now*. Which is exactly how Daddy displayed his romantic side. His proposal was out of the blue, apropos of nothing, while I was picking up around the house: "My family is coming in for Christmas, so we might as well get married." While I did appreciate the clarity and succinctness of his proposal, I felt that marriage communications should be somewhat different from campaign communications. I'm all for sound bites, and Daddy is the Zen master of sound bites (they're practical and efficient). But we both knew this situation called for a "rollout" as when candidates announce their intention to run for office.

We needed a romantic rollout! Daddy didn't disagree, he just isn't an organization man. He does strategy; let someone else figure out the tactics. If I wanted romance, I was going to have to create it, which was more practical than getting mad at him for his drive-by proposal. With the precision of precinct-level targeting, I put together a foolproof romantic proposal plan, one a monkey could implement. I designed my ring, faxed the drawing to the jeweler, FedExed the finished ring to Daddy's office, and had his secretary FedEx back Daddy's payment, wrap the ring, and set up a romantic lunch where he could pop the question properly.

Imagine my romantic nirvana when I unwrapped my beautiful ring! And Daddy was so proud of himself for pulling off such a suave lunch! We drank champagne while Daddy accepted compliments from all the waitresses on his fine taste in jewelry.

That afternoon, as I was luxuriating in my self-made romantic reality, something kept bothering me. Something was missing from the proposal. At first I couldn't see it, blinded as I was by my engagement ring. Then it came to me. What was missing from the preplanned proposal was the proposal.

Every good plan controls for contingency events. I snapped into action, making additional provisions for proposal perfection.

That weekend Daddy and I went to the stock car races. We climbed onto the hood of our pickup and, over the deafening roar of the car engines, I said to him, "Say to me, 'Mary, will you marry me?'" He did. I started crying, even though I couldn't hear a word he said on account of those car engines. However, since I *knew* what he was saying (for obvious reasons), I got the emotional punch I needed and he got yet another opportunity to pat himself on the back for his romantic acumen!

Taken at face value, our proposal may not sound romantic to you. But here's where the embracing love comes in: Daddy was so tickled by my extended stagecrafting and I was so pleased that he played along so indulgingly that to this day we still get a romantic glow thinking back on our "perfect" proposal. (We also get a good laugh at how equally weird we are.)

In sum, if you are feeling romantically disconnected, recalibrate. You've got to be practical *and* romantic to make a long-term relationship work. If your marriage is just practical, it will have no soul. If it is just romantic, it will have no stability.

You'll have to perform the same calisthenics for lifestyle accommodations. Daddy and I have had to make remarkably few adjustments to suit each others' preferences. We like the same cars, homes, vacations, interests, art, movies, people, history, travel, books, wine. Interests we don't share, we can easily enjoy without each other: politics, sports, and music.

You may be surprised to learn that of those interests we don't share, the only one that bothers me is music. Daddy checked out around Elvis. He is definitely a pre-Beatles guy, which has far too many ramifications to get into here. I will only say how strange it is to have your husband moan, *"Turn down that music!"*

Now we're up to the "I, Mommy/Daddy, take you, Mommy/Daddy, for better or for worse" part of getting married. Taking each other means knowing fully what you're getting into (or at least giving it some reflection) and making adjustments to keep taking care of each other. Some adjustments will be harder—much harder, worse than you could ever anticipate—but if you reflect on why you wanted to "take" each other in the first place, you'll plow through to the better part and be happy you did. (Even though you'll want to wring his neck.)

Let's move on to "for richer or for poorer." Here's another place where good marriages fuse the romantic and the practical. Romance will get you through the poor part. When Daddy and I met, he was living and working in a basement. He had a Murphy bed that he transformed into a desk during the day. He had no car, no TV, no clothes. When his apartment was robbed, he was so poor that there was nothing to take but a bottle of bourbon. (The burglar demonstrated his disdain for this circumstance by pooping on the floor.) I had more stuff but no savings. We were pretty pathetically financially positioned considering we were going into our forties. And our financial security wasn't going to improve, since neither of us was going to quit campaign work, which paid the bills but not much more. ***Alert: Icky statement just ahead.*** But we had each other. (You were warned.)

That's how my mom always spoke of the early years of

my parents' marriage. I remember those days of limits on everything. We were never anywhere near destitute, but money or the lack thereof framed our daily lives: leftovers, thermostat on low, used cars, hand-me-downs. Ma would shake out the sofa cushions for change to go to the movies.

By the time we were teens, my dad was in management at the steel mill and my mother was teaching cosmetology. They built out the house, got a new *and* second car, and took us out to dinner—a lot. They took up skiing and sailing. My dad surprised my mom with "cocktail rings," which were all the rage then but a really outrageous expense.

I, for one, did not miss dinners of scrambled eggs with pork and beans, but whenever my mom took trips down marriage memory lane, she'd always go to the days when "all we had was each other." So, embedded in my marriage DNA was the notion that poor was romantic.

Poor is *not* romantic. Financial insecurity tops the list of marital stresses. What *is* romantic is struggling and building a life together, sharing accomplishments and accumulating the comforts won by combined effort. My dad and your dad call this "providing for my family." Providing well is a very important validator for men. My mom (and yours) strive to "make a home," which is our validator.

Let's get to the practical part of "for richer or for poorer." Being poor is only romantic if you're working hard to stop being poor. (Some families work very hard and cannot grow out of poverty, but that's a whole other topic.)

It is true that "money can't buy you happiness" (voice of Ma), but it can get you a lot of giggles! Perhaps you've noticed the plaque I put in Daddy's bathroom: "Anyone who says money can't buy you happiness doesn't know where to shop."

It's a joke. Maybe.

Rich is relative. Each couple will define "rich" in their marriage. The important thing is that you agree on the meaning in your marriage.

For us, money does buy happiness because it calms Daddy down. He lives in a perpetual state of fear that we won't have enough for our retirement. He never wants to be a burden on his family. The more we put away, the calmer he becomes (well, calm for *him*). I like money because I need options. Money gives you the freedom to devote time to low-paying work you love and to walk away from BS situations. I crack up when I feel trapped.

So Daddy and I need a certain amount of money to mitigate our own worst fears.

But here's where "richer" can be as trying as "poorer" on a marriage. Cliché alert! Money doesn't fall off trees. Money comes from work. More work makes more money. But, cliché alert! Money is time—time not spent with your spouse. And high-paying work is also usually stressful. You take out that stress on your spouse or it leaves you distracted and distant, either of which can just tank a marriage. This is why I keep commanding you to define *rich* as "rich in love." Only you can determine how much money you need to keep your marriage romantic and practical.

Are you ready for more heavy sledding in marriage vows? Let's move on to "in sickness and in health." Don't take this too literally. It's an unfair pledge because men are born hypochondriacs. Also, when they're sick, men revert to infancy. I'm talking the sniffles here, or a toothache, or a pulled muscle. Men *love* to talk about how awful they feel and be waited on and felt sorry for.

Therefore, think of this pledge of betrothal only for serious health issues. It applies to the whole panoply of genuine sickness, including addictive behaviors (alcoholism, gambling, drugs) and mental problems (depression and the like). You are released from your pledge if (a) your mate refuses to help himself get over self-destructive diseases, or (b) he *in any way* abuses you. You two are both suckers for a sob story, but you can never help anyone who won't help himself.

Now let's talk about kids, the most precious of God's gifts. They become the raison d'être of your marriage. You become gloriously and totally enmeshed in their every movement.

This heavenly experience can be hell on a marriage.

I see my young men friends work in total tandem with their wives in child rearing. I am amazed and impressed but mostly curious. Daddy is a product of his times, and in those days child rearing was mostly mothers' duty. Daddy wouldn't even hold you until you were toddlers for fear he'd drop you or break your neck (or get spit up on). He didn't feed you, change you, bathe you, put you to sleep. Your screaming in a restaurant fell on his deaf ears. It never occurred to him to talk or rock you while I ate.

Let me make something completely clear here: I would have chopped off his hands with a butter knife if he'd tried to do any of the above. I confess to being a total control freak over you both and make no apologies for it. My attention and devotion to you was unstoppably comprehensive and absorbing, 24/7. I was so completely fulfilled and overwhelmed by my unparalleled love for you, I needed nothing else.

And gave little else.

Needless to say, this is not the ideal wifely behavior for a man who was born into and never left the center of attention. I vaguely knew I might be giving Daddy short shrift but—and this is the worst part—*I did not care.*

All I wanted was you.

Looking back, I am astounded by Daddy's endless patience, usually not one of his best traits. When I wasn't totally under your spell, I was crabby, exhausted, mindless. He put up with that too.

Which brings me to my final point, which is really my first point on marriage: understand what you're getting into. For better or for worse. Because when you get in, you gotta get in deep and completely and reliably. Even then, you have to call on your faith in a higher force to hold you when you want to run.

More often than not, my prayers are in wholehearted gratitude for the extraordinary gift of my marriage. When I ask Daddy, "Do you love me?" he answers, "I worship you; I adore you; it's not love, it's complete capitulation. I'm the most uxorious man you'll ever meet." (He loves that weird word.) This slightly overwrought expression of his affection is the Carvillian version of my response to him on the same question, which is "I dig the whole package." (Don't even *think* of making fun of our love vernacular.)

We're exchanging our appreciation for, and reaffirming our commitment to, the life we are building. The longer we build, the stronger we get. We are both stunned and humbled by our blessings.

Even with all that work, not every marriage works out. Breakups are truly sad and disorienting, even mutually desired ones. You can truly love someone, and the marriage still fails. What I think all moms want their daughters to understand is love is necessary but not sufficient for a good and lasting marriage. Making marriage work takes resolve, accommodation, and patience. Mothering can be hard work but comes so naturally you don't think about it. Marriage requires concentrated, tough effort sometimes, but when it works, it is fulfilling, inspiring, gratifying like no other experience. It makes for true contentment.

I realize with some people Daddy conjures up the image of a frog, not Prince Charming, but he is my knight in shining armor. I pray you each find your perfect Prince Charming and live happily ever after.

Love,
Mom

P.S. All this talk makes me want to go kissy-face with Daddy and make Matty say, "Yuk!" and Emma say, "Hooray!"

Myself, my father, Steven G. Matalin; "Grandma Barb"; James, Matty, Emma, and Maria Cino, 2003, retaking our wedding vows.

GRANDE DAME

Dear Cardsharks,

We play cards a lot, Go Fish, Crazy Eights, War, and our favorite, Old Maid. We try to make these almost mindless games generic teaching opportunities . . . sportsmanship, concentration, partnership, etc. I get a little carried away with Old Maid. Every time we play, I preadmonish everyone that it is impolite to call someone an old maid. But why? What's wrong with being an old maid? What does an old maid have that a young maid doesn't? In a word, marriage.

Here's what an old maid *does* have: freedom, privacy, more fun with less responsibility, mobility, tranquillity, variety. She has total and complete control of the TV remote. Nothing in her home is ever out of place, used up, or rotting under a bed. There's always gas in her car; there are never dirty dishes in her kitchen sink or whiskers in her bathroom sink. She can see any movie she wants, sleep in or stay up reading all night without disturbance. She can choose jobs, homes, cars, pets, and vacations without prolonged negotiations.

I am not attacking marriage. I just want you girls to understand there are other satisfying and fulfilling lifestyles. Marriage isn't mandatory. It's not for everybody. Some people just don't find a "till death do us part" partner.

Some might think going home to an empty house is an uncomfortable thing. Not necessarily; it can be nirvana. Yesterday I sat in Aunt Maria's fourth-floor home office while she was at work. It was completely quiet, spotless, still. It was soothing, Zenlike. I could feel my blood pressure dropping. I went there to prepare for *Meet the Press*, but I ended up happily paralyzed, unable to heave my strangely relaxed self off her overstuffed couch. I was overcome in an environment where I could actually hear, let alone think. The absence of constant commotion, interruption, distraction made me feel like I was in a different country, not merely next door.

Sitting by myself in Maria's palace made me think about the common presumption that bachelorettehood is lonely. I'm sure most single people have some lonely times, but there's plenty of loneliness in marriage too. Having a body around doesn't mean you've found another soul. Maria's never lonely. She has dozens of interests, literally hundreds of friends, and her beloved position as your honorary aunt. She has a deep Catholic faith. She travels constantly. She's happy. People are forever coming to her for solace, comfort, advice, camaraderie, and fun. I hope Daddy and I provide an attractive portrait of a marriage, but I'm so happy you have such a fine example of a successful, fulfilling life without one.

Surprisingly, my younger girlfriends feel pressured to get married today. No one ever pressured me; I think I struck people as unlikely marriage material. Even after ten years, some girlfriends still comment on my "domesticity," which they consider abnormal for me. I can't remember what it was like *not* to be married (this is some version of the Stockholm syndrome), but I don't remember feeling pressured to be married. (I do remember pressuring Daddy to "poop or get off the pot"—one of my all-time favorite momisms—when I felt it was time to get serious.) I guess I'm surprised there's any pressure on these women in the "career capitals"—big cities where opportunities are limitless and alternatives to marriage more obvious. But women who come here for professional reasons bring along their hometown personal values. Their parents and/or peers keep them ever mindful of the traditional paths.

Some of the pressure to marry is self-imposed. The dating scene is a drag for ambitious young men and women who work long hours. The old biological clock is a big pressure. Obviously companionship and kids are the most beautiful benefits of marriage, but they should come your way because you want them, God willing—not by way of artificial pressure.

As in all things, be true to yourself. Follow your own path and your own timeline. Just to remind you that there's more than one good path out there, I'm changing the rules so that whoever's holding the last old maid card is the winner—the grande dame!

XOXO,
Your Queen of Hearts

FAITH

Dear Little Ye of Faith,

When I was growing up, my parents didn't put a lot of emphasis on structured religion. Gram took me with her to a Catholic church where the mass was conducted in Croatian (Vatican II wasn't a big help in my neighborhood). I loved the rituals, the singing, the incense. I was somehow comforted by Gram's deep faith. I could tell something important was going on, but it wasn't explained to me. We grew up as "cultural Catholics," but my mom had us confirmed as Methodists when we were teens. After confirmation she said, "You pick your religion now." As a bona fide child of the sixties, I fell away from structured religion. I felt hemmed in by all those negative thou-shalt-nots. I worried that too many Western religions excluded or denigrated the role of women.

So why did I enroll you both in a religious school

where you have chapel once a week and explicitly spiritual instruction every day? Because I wanted you to have that scaffolding for a life lived with faith. Because I believe in my heart of hearts that a life without faith is unanchored and unfulfilling. Without it, you're just wandering in the desert. You experience deeply that the whole is greater than the sum of its parts when you work through a structured organization of faith. And I still think the singing is damn good.

However you want to practice your faith, I want you to believe in something way larger than yourself and to extract from that faith a strength in yourselves, a place you can go for wisdom and support, a foundation for giving back. If you get nothing else from your education, that will be more than enough.

Even though I fell away, I kept a yearning for learning more about religion and faith. At the same time, I've harbored a skepticism toward perennial "searchers"—those hot on the latest spiritual trend. To me, they range from the fashionably faithful to brainwashed cultists; faux believers. Because of either my mom's belief that religion was a personal affair or my innate midwestern reserve, I had a hard time relating to openly religious folks. But then I got a different perspective working at the White House with people of deep religious faith. They had inner peace, strength, a constant compass, tolerance, reverence, acceptance. Despair didn't exist on their radar screen. Their faith gave them a sense of fulfillment and serenity. They inspired me to reactivate my long-lost search for my faith.

In my quest, I've read a myriad of religious literature, both spiritual and academic. I've enjoyed long, provocative conversations with people of faith. Daddy is very educated on many religions and is, of course, a devout Catholic. He has been a patient guide for me. When I rail against the church, its current scandals and past discrimination, he always comes back to "you have to focus on the good." Aunt Renie is also a Catholic but has studied many philosophies, which has helped forge her Eastern meditative calmness. Your beloved Nee-Nee used to take you to the Assemblies of God church. You loved the wailing and sing-shouting, clapping, and hallelujahs. You yawned your way through mass after that! Right now I'm studying the life of Mary Magdalene and reading the Gnostic gospels. Together we will study the Bible and investigate all the world's religions; it's fascinating to see how many ways people search for God. The Gnostics thought Jesus was about a deep inner knowledge; they taught that "the light is inside of you; it's inside of everybody." There are a million ways to get that light inside of you.

I can pinpoint the very moment I first felt that light inside me. It was when I first gave birth. The event was beyond words, beyond explanations. It was a miracle. For the first time in my life, I just gave myself over to a place I couldn't explain, and accepted that I didn't need to explain it to believe in it. You can't look at your baby's face and not believe in God. Once you find that place in your heart, you find it everywhere.

I'm finding that same faith in my family, my husband, my friends. I saw it in the pervasive goodness and community following 9/11. It's not in any building; it's not on page 123 in our hymnals. The most religious experiences I've had didn't take place in any church. Years ago I'd gone on a mission to Israel with a bunch of hard-nosed politicians. In the middle of the day, we found ourselves on top of Mount Masada, where a group of Israeli musicians had also gathered. Quite spontaneously, they began to play under the hot, white, radiant sun. All the quarreling and hard feelings of the day fell away, and our group became silent, almost breathless. They stopped just as abruptly, and I walked down the steep mountainside, speechless with awe, tears rolling down my face. Inexplicably I felt we'd all been pulled into something that connected us to each other and to some higher power.

I like attending church services but I've learned that you don't need the language of any church to pray and that prayer was born to help us express thankfulness and gratitude. Every night as we sit down to eat, I ask, "What are we grateful for?" You girls immediately start pushing my buttons: "Candy!" "That we can watch TV tonight!" You know I'm gonna go nuts over those answers. I'll push a little more, then get some groans. "Oh, okay, I'm grateful for my friends." By the fourth go-round, you'll say, "I'm grateful for the gift of love, the blessing of a sister, the beautiful place where we live." We pray for our family and loved ones. We pray for our soldiers. And try as I might, I can't get Matty to stop praying for Osama. "But, Mom, he's a sick man and I'm praying that he'll get better."

I'm also teaching you to pray for help, to ask when you need something. Not for wealth but for guidance, wisdom, comfort, support, charity. This is hard for me given my midwestern stubbornness and indefatigable sense of rugged individualism. But that's what faith is: knowing that you can hit the wall and just give it up to a power greater than yourself. I'm still trying to get there, and I hope you'll join me on this quest. May your most important prayer be "I can't do this alone."

God bless,
Mom

A TIME FOR GRIEVING

Dear Girls,

Every Fourth of July, Daddy's side of the family cara-vans up from Louisiana to our farm to celebrate our nation's birth, Matty's birth, and just life in general. The Carville family needs little incentive to celebrate, but the "farm party" has, in a short time, turned into a much-anticipated, elaborately planned family tradition. We love the endless calls reporting progress from the road as the family drives in an automotive parade, calling each other on the CB radio, alternately crabbing and laughing. The dads do the driving, the "sisters" do the radio chatter. As the multiple vans, SUVs, and cars pull in the dusty farm drive, kids, food, bags, blankets, and all manner of cooking paraphernalia, including a jambalaya pot, spill out with the tumble of people. Daddy's brother-in-law Uncle Mike would never make his jambalaya in anything other than his own humongous black kettle, over which he stands in the sticky sun, stirring with a long black shovel-spoon while the wood fire blazes: we're talking *gallons* of jambalaya. Uncle Mike also insists on old hens for the savory pork, sausage, and poultry mix. Two years ago we had, Lord have mercy, Virginia chickens—*no no no!* Uncle Mike is a man of few words (rare for Cajuns), but his look of stupefaction when we produced Safeway chickens said it all. What Yankee rubes! He was too kind to actually say what his face clearly expressed. So last year we gave the always reliable Uncle Bill the very critical assignment of transporting old hens from Louisiana.

The arriving horde feels like a swarm of locusts in reverse; they totally blanket our farm with plenty, rather than strip it. Daddy's five sisters, two brothers, all their spouses, and their combined two dozen offspring—from infants to young adults—flow down the drive and swarm the house, barn, farm vehicles, pool and card tables, swimming pool, and swing set. Within ten minutes the sisters have everything put up and have assumed positions they will hold for most of the rest of the visit, with their beers, Bloody Marys, and ciggies (they call smoking "gerting"). The blackjack, bingo, and yahtzee games begin. Music blares. We chatter like magpies, catching up as if we don't talk *every single day.* Daddy brags on you girls—how special, clever, funny, smart . . . "No one loves their kids like James," the sisters say sarcastically. Daddy always misses the sarcasm and sincerely says, "That's right" every single time. (There is a lot of repetition in Carville family gatherings.) He usually throws in a "Isn't my wife beautiful? Don't I have the best wife in the world? Can you believe she's forty, forty-one, forty-two . . . ? " Daddy is a man of large appetites, limitless appreciation for life, and little modesty.

While the sisters guffaw at Daddy's endless bragging (which extends to his dogs but not to the cats, fish, turtles, or hamsters), they are kissing, hugging, proclaiming, "Look at you!", while they pass you both around as enthusiastically as they did when you both were newborns. I always grab the latest babies. There's always a chubby-cuddle available in the nonstop-growing Carville clan.

Serious effort and considerable competition attend any and all interactions—cards, baseball, paintball, racing the four-wheeler through the muddy pastures, cocktail making, and disc spinning. Among the roughest competitions is the limbo contest. Aunt Pat always controls the music. The limbo stick (aka broom handle) is scrupulously monitored for consistency among contestants. This event generally follows or accompanies the beer-chugging contest. Your Aunt Maria usually wins, most amazingly without pouring suds down her chest. Cousin Keith, the super-athlete, is a frequent limbo victor, but last year Riley (our longtime friend/babysitter/intern/and all-around great person from the Valley) kicked butt!

Matty's birthday-cake-candle-blowing sing-a-thon is

another pivotal event. By that time all are clamoring for their pointy, elastic-banded birthday hats; weirdly, the men leave theirs on after the big blow!

The festivities continue all night long. Someone always gets hurt; no one doesn't have fun.

Uncle Bill, Daddy's younger brother by six years, has always been a star of the show. Everyone loves Uncle Bill. He was a loner until marrying Aunt Holly last year, but he was never alone. He would show up at our home for no reason at any time and just grab a couch. You girls were smitten with him from the time you could talk and walk, and we love watching the home movies of our July Fourth gatherings with his silly narration: "And here's Emma/Matty, isn't she something? *Say* something!"

Bill undertook his assignment to fetch old hens for the jambalaya with a conscientiousness and seriousness of purpose akin to a soldier under fire (which he was in Vietnam, where he saw many buddies blown to bits). We knew he'd come through; Bill wasn't in the habit of letting people down. His last all-consuming goal had been to quit drinking before his mama died, the amazing, legendary Miss Nippy. With the help of his always-there family and AA, he did it. His next goal was to fulfill his mama's dream for him to find a good woman to love and marry. He did that too, last year. So we were all looking forward to Uncle Bill's driving in the Carville caravan to our Fourth of July celebration with his wonderful new wife, Holly. Then, horribly, just a few miles from the farm, Uncle Bill had a heart attack and died almost immediately.

All of us were in total shock. We canceled Matty's eighth birthday party and the rest of the celebration and numbly prepared for a funeral instead. You were both stunned, enraged. You look forward to the family party from Christmas on and talk about it for the rest of the year. You don't understand losing a loved one, not like you understood shutting down that once-a-year blowout.

For being so young, you've lost too many, too unexpectedly, in shockingly random and abrupt ways. Our beloved caregiver from Matty's birth, your cooing comfort zone and my surrogate mama, was "under the weather" one week and gone the next. (She'd sworn the lump she'd had removed a few months earlier had been nothing.) We never had the chance to say good-bye. This hard loss followed immediately on the heels of the unfathomable loss of some classmates' family members in the 9/11 attack on Washington. Out of the blue, a beloved school principal suffered a stroke and perished. A young, super class mom with three babies under five, including a newborn, had been laughing at school on a Friday, as always, and was dead of an aneurysm that Sunday. Then Uncle Jim's mom, Daddy's mom, and daddy's surrogate father, Uncle Lloyd, passed. Whenever the phone rings at an odd time, I tense up and you pick up on it.

You do understand your parents in pain. It terrifies you.

Whenever I look remotely sad, you say, "Did somebody die?" Worse, when I get even a cold, you panic. "Mommy, I don't want you to die!" When you say that to me, *I* panic. I freeze. I still say the same thing to myself about my mother in moments of despair or dark dreams. I don't know if I'll ever come to terms with losing my mother. The thought of your having that kind of pain motivated me to help you face death with some clarity, so I can comfort you—and more important, so you can learn how to comfort yourselves.

I missed an opportunity to show you the ways of comforting when I kept you from Uncle Bill's funeral. Looking back, I think, this was a mistake, but at the time I just didn't know how scary it would have been for you to see Daddy so profoundly disconsolate, in such uncontrollable sorrow. On the other hand, that funeral would have shown you how to grieve, explained why it's important to grieve, and demonstrated that grieving together is a powerfully healing experience. The mass was truly supportive and restorative. Most of Uncle Bill's two dozen nieces and nephews contributed to the service, and Uncle Steve's eulogy really captured the Bill so beloved by that packed church. You couldn't help feeling uplifted. You couldn't stop feeling glad we had had Bill. And that much deep, true love in one place made you absolutely certain that Bill was now in peace.

Back at Aunt Mary Ann's home, there was so much buttery southern food, such a free-flowing, elbow-lifting bar crowd, and so many merry Bill stories, we could have been at the family farm party. We laughed as much as we cried. We celebrated as we grieved.

Daddy talks to one or several of his remaining six siblings just about every day about Uncle Bill, and they are each coming to their own peace.

Girls, I don't know any way to explain death to you. I can tell you there is no answer to the "Why?" question: why your loved one; why now; why in such a way.

I've asked the "Why?" question too hard for too long, and now I just have a big unanswered hole instead of some peace. So skip the "Why?" and go to the "What?" and "Who?" Who really was the precious person? What did she love and what did you love about her?

The "How?" question is tough, as in "How am I supposed to deal with this?" Our friend, your "uncle" Tim Russert, the journalist, once passed on the only answer that ever gave me any hope of resolving that question. A colleague of ours had lost his son in a senseless tragedy. Tim spoke to the father, who couldn't imagine going on without his boy. "Ask yourself this: Would your life have been better without him? Would you have been willing to miss what you had to be free of this pain now?" Hearing these loving questions posed with such clarity from such a devoted son and doting father of a son hit home hard and true.

When the hard time comes and you lose someone you love, I hope you'll ask yourselves these questions. And I hope you won't ask them in isolation. Please don't grieve alone. Aunt Renie, Aunt Maria, and all the Carville aunts are really giant, soft bosoms of comfort. You will find the joy of sharing memories of the one you love a healing balm for the pain of loss. Mark the passing of those you loved with a big old blowout, bigger than the Fourth of July party. As big as your love is deep.

In the meantime, mark the passing of *every* day with those you love with love.

Forever and ever and always,

Mom

SEALED WITH A KISS

Dear Once and Future Correspondents,

There is no greater keepsake than letters. Old letters transport you with pinpoint precision to a certain time, place, and state of mind. You'll never be able to remember events and emotions as poignantly as you can easily chronicle them at the time. Even nonevents, maybe *especially* nonevents, are special places in retrospect when you capture them contemporaneously.

Diaries can be interesting histories but by definition are one-sided. Correspondence, by definition, is connection to another, which requires empathy and, hopefully, coherence. It isn't mandatory to string your thoughts together with any semblance of sanity in your own diary. Letters have the potential, at the very least, to produce a modicum of coherent thought.

The very best histories are the ones drawn from letters, especially family letters. Promise you'll read Queen Victoria's letters to her daughters.

I'm no good at letters because my hand is too slow for my hyper, free-floating thoughts. When I slow my brain down to keep up with my hand, the result is ramble. Daddy has an even harder time getting his racing, ricocheting thoughts through a writing process he finds sluggish and cumbersome. He makes up for it in verbalization. He's a verbal hailstorm. Only twice in twelve years have I felt the need to have him slow it down and soften it up and write me a letter. Once for a birthday in 1992; again in 2003 for our tenth anniversary. His written expression, not to mention his handwriting, is like a carton of fishing bait. It's a bunch of moving squiggles: you know it's alive and tasty to its intended audience, but you'd just rather have the fish. He doesn't like reading letters either. It's a shame he doesn't want to "fool with" computers (he calls the internet "the interstate") because he has an attention span born for e-mail speed. E-mail is manna from heaven for the letter-writing challenged.

It's trendy to lament the rise of e-mail and the alleged demise of letters as literature, but I think e-mail is a boon to those short on attention and long on sarcasm, which is practically every friend I have—especially mothers. The immediacy of electronic communications is motivating in ways that letter writing isn't. It's also an intrinsic smart-aleck instigator, and this can really get you smiling through the day.

The point here is to communicate. Connect. Chronicle. Preserve. It doesn't matter whether it's by letters, e-mail, cards, videotape. Draw pictures. Photos count, but they're no substitute for your unique expressions. I have—and I am not exaggerating—dozens of supersized Tupperware barrels filled with family photos, but none compares with the finger painting Matty did of me when she was in kindergarten. Two blue rectangles drip from my hands; Matty says the painting is me getting ready to pick up dog poo.

Emma, the second word you learned to write after your own name was MOM. For months I got "letters" every day from you: EMMA ❤ MOM. I saved every one.

In fact, I've saved practically every scrap of paper either of you has laid hands on since your first crayon experience. Every drawing, cutout, letter book, and finger painting is boxed and labeled and stored. Everywhere. Even our guest tub is filled with boxes! Yes, these paper mountains are potential fire hazards, but they preserve for all time a point in time, your place in time. They are a prelude to your own "letter collections."

You'll treasure my obsessive collecting in the future, as I treasure all the letters my sister has saved from our college years. I yearn for tangible remembrances from our earlier years, but there are none. They were lost or tossed when Ma died. She wasn't much of a saver to start with and less of a writer. It really bothers me that I don't have a single letter from my mother. It's a regret you won't have.

You'll never regret writing any letter out of love. However, it's a good idea to reread anything you've written in anger, angst, or (God forbid) inebriation. Maybe hold on to it for a day or two before sending it. Or write it for the cathartic value, then destroy it. In my business, where everything is liable to subpoena, I've been embarrassed more than once by having sent letters written in haste and without reflection.

When it comes to your family and friends, write even when you have nothing in particular to say. Make your letters long, short, silly, serious, happy, despondent. Just stay connected.

This book started out as a way to connect you to your roots, to pass along bits of family wisdom. Mostly I wanted you to know my mom. As is often the case when you struggle to convey your truest thoughts in writing, I came to know my mother and what it means to be a mother in ways and with emotions I had never known. Rereading this long love letter, the words don't seem to adequately express the extent to which I learned how linked together we all are . . . what mother-daughter love is. But writing it crystallized that bright truth so clearly, so tangibly for me that I can almost hold it in my hands. So what started out as a keepsake for you became a key to many insights for me.

There is much more to tell and, I suspect, to discover, my darling lambs. I hope these letters will serve as a beginner's guide to life's many mysteries and joys. May you receive them and keep them in the spirit they were intended. Sealed with a kiss,

> With love forever and always for all time,
> XOXO,
> Mom

ABOUT THE AUTHOR

Mary Matalin has served as Assistant to President George W. Bush and Counselor to Vice President Dick Cheney. Matalin held senior positions in the 1988 and 1992 national campaigns for President George H.W. Bush ('41). She hosted CNN's *Crossfire*, was a founding cohost of *Equal Time*, and recently starred in Steven Soderbergh and George Clooney's *K Street*. She also coauthored with her husband, James Carville, the best-selling *All's Fair: Love, War, and Running for President*. She and Carville reside in Virginia with their daughters, Matalin "Matty" Carville and Emerson "Emma" Normand Carville, as well as three dogs, four cats, two hamsters, and several turtles (two of which coincidentally are ingredients in her husband's gumbo). At PTA meetings she is known to remind people that she is an expert on children with attention deficit hyperactivity disorder, having married one in 1993.